Rez
Salute

Rez
Salute
The Real
Healer Dealer

Jim Northrup

FULCRUM
GOLDEN, COLORADO

Text © 2012 Jim Northrup

Library of Congress Cataloging-in-Publication Data
Northrup, Jim, 1943-
  Rez salute : the real healer dealer / Jim Northrup.
    p. cm.
  ISBN 978-1-55591-762-3 (pbk.)
  1. Northrup, Jim, 1943- 2. Ojibwa Indians--Biography. 3. Ojibwa Indi-ans--Social life and customs. 4. Fond du Lac Indian Reservation (Minn.)--Social life and customs. 5. Ojibwa wit and humor. I. Title.
  E99.C6N68 2012
  305.897--dc23

                              2012015997

Printed in the United States of America
0 9 8 7 6 5 4 3 2 1

Design by Jack Lenzo

Fulcrum Publishing
4690 Table Mountain Dr., Ste. 100
Golden, CO 80403
800-992-2908 • 303-277-1623
www.fulcrumbooks.com

To Umpa Owaastewii and Giiwedin Noodin

Contents

Foreword by Margaret Noori .... *xi*

Preface: Fond du Lac Follies and a Writer's Life ....*xvii*

1. This Way Niswi—2002... 1
2. Bundles Is One Year Young—2003......................... 23
3. Moose Alert on Northrup Road—2004................... 45
4. Enough for a Shinnob, Not Enough for a
   Chimook—2005.. 59
5. Just Make Everyone Four-Fourths—2006.............. 75
6. Pretending to Be Actors—2007 89
7. The Results Were Not So Pretty Good—2008 109
8. We Laughed Muchly—2009................................. 139
9. Wife for Life Patricia—2010 171
10. Tickled a Little Moo Out of Me—2011 195

About the Author *221*

Foreword

Ishgonigan Anamikan: Rez Salute

Rez Salute! The title suggests standing up, taller than usual, taking off your hat, and looking once in each direction: east, south, north, and west. *Ishgonigan Anamikan! Ahow! Ahow! Ahow! Ahow!* In Anishinaabemowin, the language Jim Northrup uses like a strong rope to cast an anchor into the future, *Rez Salute* is *Ishgonigan Anamikan. Ishgonigan* is a word that means "the thing after, the leftovers, the remains." Jim invites readers to experience his Rez as a maamakaaj place, where days are sometimes easy, sometimes entertaining, and always worth remembering. What Jim does is share his reverence for history, for stories, and for the place where he has centered his voice for more than half a century and where the voices of his relatives stretch into the distant past and the faraway future. Native American fiction and nonfiction is sometimes assigned a tragic ending in which the subject disappears into the sunset, merging with the land that was the object of colonial desire. Jim offers an alternative to this type of ending. His book has no bowed rider at the end of the trail. It is a proud salute to many nations, those to which he belongs and those he visits and considers united by traditions of humor, storytelling, and survival.

Anishinaabe Syndicated, the first collection of Jim's Fond du Lac Follies column, takes readers from 1989 to 2001. It coveres the early years of Jim's career and included the defense of sovereign rights, the creation of casino culture, and the simultaneous loss of and struggle to revitalize the Anishinaabe language. *Rez Salute*, the second collection of the same column, picks up the trace of lessons and stories in 2002 and spans another decade. Readers will recognize the same characters, the same shores and trees, the same nation and politicians, the same seasons and traditions. Yet *Rez Salute* resonates the way a bell rung many years might, the way an older eagle might circle land he knows well.

Bears still track through town, but Sawyer has a new community center for storytelling, healing, and gathering. At the casino, where Jim's wife, Pat, won the finicky but fabulous '64 Corvette Sting Ray, things are getting more commercial, but the buffet is amazing and the new hotel is helpful when visitors to Northrup Road are too numerous. And the visitors do occasionally overflow. The World Headquarters of the Fond du Lac Follies has always been global, but this book documents the way it has changed from a chance destination where an unknown journalist got his start to the place pilgrims find an award-winning poet, columnist, and novelist. Jim still recounts the significant elections on and off the Rez, but he also finds himself, and his friends and family, connecting with Hollywood. In 2006, an entire crew showed up and cast a few characters (and his fire pit) in a scene. Although he seasons the years with his inimitable humor and provocative questions, his representation of these times is important. These chapters are not Jim's memoirs; they are the wisely edited recollection of significant events in Anishinaabe history. Jim's version of many events stands as counterpoint to versions presented by mainstream media. As non-Native and Native historians return to these years, his words will be a valuable resource for understanding how he saw the world as both a member of the Fond du Lac Band of Lake Superior Chippewa and a Marine who served the United States in Vietnam.

Beyond the changing history of nations, Jim writes of seasonal and generational cycles. Ricing and work in the sugar bush happen again and again, but the babies become the kids who become the masters of these arts eventually. In 2002 he writes, "My grandson Ezigaa led the way into the woods. He carried the drill. Right away he started doing the maple tree dance." By 2009 he starts the season with "a good-well trained crew . . . my sons, Jim, Matthew, Joe, Aaron Ezigaa, and Calvin . . . also my nephew Kris and daughter-in-law Jackie." His family is growing and his years of patient teaching pay off as he explains, "My part was easy. All I did was sit and lip point at what I wanted done next. At the end of the day my lips were just tired." Clearly, he is passing on tradition, but he is passing on much more than skills and activities. His gift for storytelling and wry humor ripple into the next generation. With the ease of the eagles he mentions, he moves from a serious reference to the sap as "a gift from the Creator" to a chuckle and an aside telling readers, "My son Aaron asked if I could move my chair and supervise from 'way the hell over there,' out of the way. I complied."

Jim teaches all of us to pay attention, to enjoy life, to not shy away from the truth . . . to salute the lives before us and prepare for the lives that will follow. He doesn't lean on adjectives or superlatives. He talks about nature, but as part of a complex and relationship, not merely the object of worship. He talks about hard times and difficulty, but only so that he can better understand the lessons of events and share stories of survival. He may have a reservation to write from, but Jim Northrup has no reservations.

I have had the honor of knowing Jim for many years, and I have seen many mornings with him as he opens his palm, offers a bit of tobacco, and greets the morning. Some days I take time to say those same words in Anishinaabemowin, and whether I am at his side or on the other side of the lakes, I find strength and comfort in his salute to the day. Writing this foreword I was reminded that in Anishinaabemowin the word *anami'aa* (to pray) sounds very much like *anamikaa* (to salute). G'miigwechin. G'miigwewigo. Jim g'kinomaaimin pii dibaajomoyin / you teach us all with your stories. In return I offer a poem:

Ishgonigan Anamikan / Rez Salute
    Pii ishgoniganong ishkwaa / When you are on the Rez, after
        nigaangaabawiyin giizisoon / you stand before the sun
        anamikaman giizhigad / you salute the day
        anamikaman zhingwaakwag / you salute the pines
        anamikaman kina gaa ezhiwebag / you salute all that has happened
        dash gii anamikaman Gwaaba'iganing. / you salute the village where you live.
        Epiichi anami'aayin / And while you pray
        anaami-giizhigong / beneath the wide sky

anamikawadwa niniijaanisag / you salute the children
anamikawadwa nooshishenyag / you salute the
grandchildren
anamikawadwa zhimaaganishag / you salute the soldiers
dash anamikawadwa Anishinaabeg / you salute all
Anishinaabe people.
Kinomawadwa maampii akiing / You teach everyone
here, on earth
ji-zoongidiwaad ji-anamikawaad. / to stay strong, to
salute.
Ahow . . . ahow . . . ahow . . .ahow.

Preface

Fond du Lac Follies and a Writer's Life

When I began to write the Fond du Lac Follies, I had no idea I was writing history. I just wanted to write a column where I had freedom of speech. The Indian Civil Rights Act gave me freedom of speech, but the tribal governments made sure through various nefarious means it couldn't be exercised. We don't have free speech on my Reservation.

So I wanted to write a column that was free of the taint of government interference. I like that no one can tell me what to write about.

For the past twenty years, I have enjoyed being the fella that writes the Follies. Since the column carries my picture, people get a monthly reminder of what I look like. As I travel about, people always come up to tell me they liked what I wrote. And that is why I keep writing.

—Jim Northrup, 2012
Northrup Road, Sawyer, Minnesota

Chapter 1

This Way Niswi—2002

Flags, flags, and more American flags. I see the red-white-and-blue of the flags almost everywhere I go. The Fond du Lac Reservation gave black nylon jackets to all of the veterans from the Rez. On the left sleeve is an American flag. I have been proudly wearing that jacket for four years or more. The flag symbolizes my time in Vietnam. I remember the flag-draped caskets coming home from that war. As a young Marine, I was taught to salute the American flag to show respect. I remember how to do a proper hand salute. The right arm is held at a forty-five-degree angle, fingers extended and joined, touching the right eyebrow or hat brim. The salute is held then cut away smartly. I salute American flags. Lately, it has been getting out of hand. I was used to rendering a hand salute when I drove by a Perkins restaurant or some used-car lots, but now my arm is getting sore with all this saluting. Salute, salute, salute. I once counted fifty-six salutes as I drove through the downtown area of a small town in Minnesota. The flags were on every light pole. I don't drive that way anymore. I got some bananas at the store, and each one had a tiny American flag sticker on the side of the peel. The terrorists who attacked America are going to be very afraid now that we have flags on our bananas. As for me, I am going bananas saluting bananas. There are flags on fence posts in the middle of nowhere. I see American flag billboards and decals and small ones waving from vehicles on the highways of America. I have seen Christmas lights turned into our national symbol. I am going into a flag overload. On the Rez, the treatment center in Sawyer has a novel way of displaying the red-white-and-blue. Here the flag is tied just to the top grommet. The flag stands straight out when the wind is blowing.

I walked through the Black Bear Casino parking lot. I could see bits of patriotism sprinkled about, radio antenna flags, decal flags, and window sticker flags. When I got inside, Mike Himango, the casino manager, gave me a small American flag pin. He said all of the employees are wearing them. The flag was made in China.

In the casino gift shop, I saw more examples of patriotism/commercialism. It is hard to tell the difference when saluting key chains, refrigerator magnets, buttons, pins, and even a car air freshener. As a veteran of the Vietnam War, I wished I could have seen so many flags when I came home.

This is what we are doing to combat terrorism on this part of the Reservation. If we didn't do it this way, then the terrorists will have won (Fond du Lac Follies' favoritest cliché).

Niswi we call him. He is called so because he is the third Joe Northrup in family history. He is one month shy of the Terrible Twos and has been hanging out at the World Headquarters of the Fond du Lac Follies. He is almost tall enough to reach the doorknobs.

One sunny afternoon he was staring at Elmo on TV, the VCR had been on all morning, the tape ran as he played in the living room. I had spent seven grueling hours listening to that *Sesame Street* tinny voice and maniacal laughter. I decided to go for a walk with that little boy. I don't know why or how, but he looks like a little Irishman. His smiler works real good and he knows it. His mother dressed him for outside and we left. I carried him down the stairs so we could get outside quicker. As soon as we were out the door, he started wiggling. He wanted to be put down on the snow.

It was bright, sunny, and cool outside, no wind. The sun was shining down the road. We began the walk. He takes tiny four-inch steps, many, many of them. His steps are as long as his shoes. I held his hand until his glove came off, then I was leading him by a string. I walked him around the driveway once to get him used to following me.

I heard myself saying, "This way, Niswi, this way Niswi." With the bright sun behind us, we shadow played. Both of us waved our arms and legs about. Sure enough, the shadows did everything we did. This playing made both of us laugh out loud. He learned the meaning of "Car! Get off the road!"

The boy and I walked off the blacktop of Northrup Road into the woods. Niswi used one word out of the two hundred he knows to describe what he saw . . . stick. There were sticks all over the woods. He sampled several before he found one he liked, one that fit his little hand. Niswi drew lines in the snow with his stick, then he slashed it around like a saber.

He continued following me. It was hard walking in the woods with tiny four-inch steps, so I got ahead of him on the trail. I got far enough ahead, and then I stepped behind some trees. I wanted to see what he would do when he found himself alone in the woods. He just followed my tracks to where I was hiding.

Niswi tipped over and used his bare hands to push himself back upright. He did not like the feel of cold, wet snow on his hands. He stared at them. I warmed his hands up with mine, and we continued walking. We turned around and walked home together, smiling. I estimate we walked about a quarter mile. That is many, many four-inch steps.

I felt good inside because I had walked outside with that boy. When we got home, Niswi went to take a nap, and I hid the Elmo tape.

Dash Iskigamiziganing
Nimbiindaakoojige
Ninga-naadoobii iwidi noopiming wayiiba.
Aaniin apii waa-ozhiga'igeyan iwidi Gwaaba'iganing dash.
Mii bijiinag i'iw apii baadaajimowaad aandegwag dash.
Mii zhigwa oshki-ziigwang.
Aaniin dash apane wenji-izhichigeyan i'iw dash.
Apane nimishoomisiban apane gii-izhichige dash.
Awenen ge-wiidookawik iskigamizigeyan dash.
Indinawemaaganig miinawaa dash niwiijiiwaagan dash.
Awenen waa-mawadisik iskigamizigeyan dash.
Awegwen iidog dash.

Aaniin dash apane wenji-izhichigeyan dash.
Niniijaanisag miinawaa dash. Noozhishenyag miinawaa
dash akina.
Anishinaabeg niigaan igo ani-nitaa-iskigamizigewag dash.
Awegonen waa-aabajitooyan iwidi iskigamiziganing dash.
Ninga abaji'aag asema dash ininaatigoog dash
bagone'igan dash.
Negwaakwaanan dash ziinzibaakwadwaaboo dash
iskigamiziganaak dash.
Okaadakik dash misan dash.
Iskigamigani-ishkode dash zhingobaandag dash.
Dibaajimowinan dash.
Mii iw. Mii sa iw.

We tapped maple trees again. I like the warm sun and
the cool wind at this time of the year. In my family it is
an annual tradition. This year we have 200 taps in the
trees, but are bragging 250. My grandson Ezigaa led the
way into the woods. He carried the drill. Right away
he started doing the maple tree dance. He saw a good
tree, then another one. He looked some more and found
another good one, with one more right beside it. He was
twisting and turning in the snow looking at trees.

After an offering of tobacco, the young Shinnob
looked closer at the tree. He studied the bark, gazed
up at the branches. He looked over his shoulder to see
where the sun was and selected a place to drill the tree.
As he was drilling the tree, I thought this was the first
time he has done this part of gathering maple sap.

I was grampa proud as I am every time he does

something like this with me. I like to think he is learning things he can teach his grandchildren. Then I realized that this boy has been going to the sugar bush every year of his life.

When he was really small, I carried him to the woods so he could take part in the seasonal activity. I remember one year he was watching the eagles fly by while I was getting him out of his car seat. When he first went to school, he discovered he could run on top of the crust while the heavier adults broke through the knee-deep snow.

He has helped every year in the sugar bush. His favorite part is running from tree to tree collecting sap. Once I heard him telling his younger cousin to be careful when carrying the sap. He listens to the stories told during sugar bush. Ezigaa has his own stick for working with the fire.

One year he showed some older children how to gather dry wood for fire because they were going to camp at the sugar bush. Another year he took his new snowshoes out for a test walk. Aaron Ezigaa always helps me welcome people to the sugar bush.

One time he was keeping the Reservation Head Start kids from getting too close to the fire and the boiling kettle of sap. He put a rope on the ground around the fire pit, and then he told the younger ones no one could step across the rope but him.

There are always visitors to the sugar bush, and this year started off with a friend from Lower Michigan. Megan brought her daughter, Shannon, and her parents, Alice and Terry. I put them to work right away. We found a tree that still had a tap in it from some previous sugar bush. Megan thought it looked like a little boy tree.

It wasn't until we had tapped forty to fifty trees that I learned Asmat is related to the former king of Afghanistan Zahir Shah. I didn't know I had real royalty tapping trees with me. He seemed very eager to learn. We tapped trees all afternoon.

One afternoon my son Matthew and horseshoe partner Pea and I tapped trees. While we were bent down looking at the trees, Pea was looking at the sky. He saw one eagle, and as we looked up we saw another one. It always feels good to have eagles around.

My son Jim built a sugar shack for boiling sap. The frame is made from cedar trees that were cut to make the new golf course near the casino. My son Joseph has the dry firewood cut, split, and stacked. Jim built a fireplace for the huge stainless steel kettle he had made locally. The fireplace is brick, and Jim used clay from this Reservation to line the fire pit. He is ready to boil the sap I deliver to the sugar shack.

Question: What did Ezigaa ask for at breakfast?
Answer: Salt taagan and Gaa-wiisa pepper.

Fond du Lac Follies motored to Stevens Point, Wisconsin, and I couldn't help but wonder who the hell Stevens was and how come he gets a point? While I was at the university, I met Andy Gokee. It has been years since our moccasins were on the same trail. We ate and visited, and as I was leaving Andy gave me a gift. It was a lacrosse stick made of ash. Andy said he learned how to make them from his dad. According to Andy, the game is coming back to this area. He is doing his part by making these beautiful, functional, well-crafted lacrosse sticks.

While I was at the University of Wisconsin at Stevens Point, I recited poetry and read prose as part of Native American Month, or maybe it was Native American Week? Once again, I think every month is our month.

While on routine patrol at the junkyard, a Fond du Lac Reservation policeman saw a Toyota truck go west on Highway 210. It was about 1:00 AM when the policeman began to follow the truck.

Charlie Tuna was driving the truck with cousin Jim LeGrew riding. When Charlie saw the police car behind him, he hoped he wasn't speeding because the speedometer in the truck didn't work. Charlie continued home with the Rez police right behind him. On Maple Drive, about three miles from when they first saw each other, the police turned on their red lights and shined the spotlights into the truck. Charlie stopped and began to cooperate with the Rez police.

The policeman took Charlie's driver's license and insurance information, instructing Charlie to stay in the truck. Charlie asked why he was stopped, and the police officer informed him it was for speeding back on Highway 210.

On the way to return Charlie's license, the police officer did a plain-view search of the truck bed. He saw fish spears. He then opened a bag in the back of the truck and saw fish. He asked what kind they were. Charlie told him the fish were speared in Lake Superior and were to be used in a ceremony and to feed some elders.

The policeman asked if Charlie had any weapons besides the spears. Charlie mentioned the little knife that he uses for cleaning his fingernails. The police officer wanted to see that and then confiscated that knife, which had a two-inch blade.

After a long time sitting on the dark road, the policeman came back and told Charlie they were going to take his fish and spears. Charlie offered to clean them before they did that, but the policeman said no, they would take care of it.

Charlie drove home and the police left with the spears and fish.

Charlie went to the police and got his knife back before the case went to tribal court.

The case moved from Maple Drive to the court. After a hearing, many months passed by and occasionally Charlie thought about his fish. Finally one day, some four months after the original stop, Charlie got his fish back.

I saw the returned fish. There were seven fish in a white plastic sack, appearing to be frozen into a ball shape. Charlie is thinking of having the Rez biologists test the fish for mercury, PCBs, and other contaminants. Charlie did not get a ticket for speeding and that was the original reason for the flashing red lights. Were the police on a fishing expedition here?

The sugar bush is starting to run slow now. I think we will make our last boil soon. I haven't heard the frogs yet, so my taps are still in the trees.

This has been an interesting season with international visitors. Francois, the French chef, brought his brother from Marseilles, France. We put them to work chopping wood. Francois also brought Satchiko and Wentaro, Japanese students from Minneapolis. They helped with cutting dry wood. We learned that Satchiko is a flamenco dancer, but we didn't see her dance.

Then, of course, there was Asmat from Afghanistan. He tapped trees. Meli, a TV journalist, came from Macedonia to the sugar bush. He drank some sap, and I forgot to tell him about the dribble jug. He wore sap on his jacket when he left Sawyer. Finally, Kentaro from Japan and Mikhail from the Netherlands visited us at the World Headquarters of the Fond du Lac Follies on Northrup Road. Waffles anyone?

Question: Are you related to him?
Answer: He is my second to the last cousin.

I peeled birch bark for the first time this season. Seems like just last week I was wading in the snow at the sugar bush. It is a bit early, but when I take my time, the bark comes off in a large sheet. It is like I have to coax it to leave the tree and travel with me. Once again, Ezigaa, my now-twelve-year-old grandson, and I will be in the woods looking for bark for our baskets. We are living another seasonal cycle on this Rez. I have been spending a lot of time walking in the woods looking for birch bark so I can make fanning baskets for wild rice. It is like something or someone is guiding me to places where I can find good bark. After almost twenty years of making those baskets, called nooshkaachinaagan, I think I am getting good at it. Over the years I have made every mistake possible and have learned how to fix them. Every year people come to learn how to make them. I am glad to share what I have learned. I wish I had been paying more attention when my grampa was making them. Perhaps I could have avoided some of the mistakes.

This is about driving a Corvette. As some may recall, my wife won a '64 Corvette in a drawing at the Black Bear Casino last year. The engine is a newer Corvette engine. My friend Ray calls it an L-88 engine. The car was in storage over the winter, and it is now back on the road. My son Matthew and I picked up the car in the Cities. It just needed a jump start, and soon the motor was rumbling. We took the top down and looked cool in the Corvette for about thirty miles. Then the pretty sports car died, and I could not get it started again. We rented a dolly and loaded the car onto the unit. That damned car even looked good sitting on the dolly.

The car was dragged home, where it became a very expensive lawn ornament. I looked at it for two days, and my ace mechanic, brother-in law John Fineday, thought it needed a new module inside the distributor cap. The car is so exotic we had to order the part, and it arrived in a couple of days. That little bit of plastic and wire came to more than sixty bucks. High maintenance, indeed.

My friend Walter and I replaced the module. I got behind the wheel and tried to start it. No go, no fire to the spark plugs. Now what? We checked and the car was delivering gasoline. We inspected the coil and saw a tiny, tiny wire that was broken. I made the necessary repairs, and I got behind the wheel again. This time it fired up.

Walter and I took it for a ride. It was scary fast, I thought. I drove around town to visit my relatives and friends. I gave everyone a ride who wanted one and let some of them drive this true American sports car. All of the drivers said it was too fast for them. Some of my older relatives wouldn't even get in for a ride.

After several days of driving that sports car around, I decided it was too much car for me. So, for anyone interested, I have a '64 Corvette for sale. It has had almost thirty-five hundred dollars worth of repair work done on it. I am easy to find. I am the guy always coming out of the auto parts store.

Question: How did you know he liked powwows?
Answer: He sets up camp on Wednesday.

A long time ago, back when dinosaurs stalked the earth, I was a teenager. I attended Brainerd Indian Training School in Hot Springs, South Dakota. The school was operated by the Wesleyan Methodist Tribe. The lead dog at the school was a man named William D. Gale. President Gale was there to minister to the godless heathens.

As I recall, our weeks went like this: church three hours on Sunday morning, three hours Sunday evening, an hour of chapel every day, and a three-hour prayer meeting on Wednesday evenings.

Some forty years later I got a call from President Gale. Uh-oh, do I still owe him some demerits? The school had a policy of merits and demerits. For example, if one could memorize Bible verses and recite them, merits were earned. If one acted like a teenager, demerits were issued. I left the school under a dark cloud, one of the unsaved ones. I may still owe demerits.

It turns out Brother Gale was passing through and wanted to stop in Sawyer and visit me. He stopped and I wasn't at home. He left some copies of a book he had written called *I Sat Where They Sat*. In the book, Brother Gale reveals how he got the name Chief Hugs Himself. I sat down and began to read and got as far as the Indian Ten Commandments.

1. Thou shalt not throw bottles and cans on the road or leave junky cars in the yard.
2. Thou shalt not use a siphon hose as a credit card.
3. Thou shalt not borrow money from the paleface without paying back.
4. Thou shalt not go to rodeos or powwows . . .

I couldn't read anymore. I took that book outside and shot it. Okay, so give me more demerits.

Question: Where do you find good birch bark for baskets? Answer: Usually just on the other side of those No Trespassing signs.

Fond du Lac Follies has been dragging the family to powwows. My wife, Pat, jingle dress dances or has a food stand. Grandson Ezigaa just wanders around doing twelve-year-old kid stuff. He likes being able to do what he wants when he wants. I like the visiting that goes on and on at such places. I don't feel racism when at a powwow. I like that feeling of being a part of something interesting, a skin thing. One of my favorite parts is hearing stories from people about what is happening near them. For example, a friend reports that the elderly housing unit on his reservation is commonly called the Wrinkle Ranch. That same friend tells me about that generic toilet paper, the one that comes in the yellow-and-black packaging. It seems an Indian guy complained to the store manager about that no-name product. He even suggested a name for it. He said, call it John Wayne toilet paper. When asked why, he replied, "It is rough and tough and don't take no crap off Indians."

Question: What do you use for streetlights in Sawyer?
Answer: The stars and, once in a while, the moon.

Bears. We are seeing more bears than usual around this neck of the Rez. One black bear found my brother's garbage and scattered stuff all over the yard. My neighbor next door had his garbage scattered around. The Rez game wardens have placed a trap there. If they are successful, the bear will be transported deep into the woods. I hear of more and more bear sightings. I have seen them crossing the highways. I was driving on the interstate near Scanlon, Minnesota, when I saw a bear crossing the freeway. He almost made it, loped halfway, and was then hit by the car in front of me. His body slid off the road in a long slide. I stopped for a closer look. This was an unusual bear; in the middle of his chest there was a V shape of white hair. I have never seen that in a black bear from around here.

My aunt Beeb (Florence Greensky) said her dad told her that this is a bear highway; the bears use trails that pass through Sawyer. One summer a few years back, the kids came running in the house yelling about bears. I looked out the window and, sure enough, saw three bears strolling through the freshly mowed grass. I thought they were a mother and two babies. The bears were just walking along sniffing things. I stood on the back porch above the bears and told them to get out of here because they were scaring the kids. The bears looked at me. I said something similar in Ojibwemowin to the bears and they took off running. They left me there scratching my head thinking that bears must understand our language. Makwa niin nindoodem.

Fond du Lac Follies motored to Danbury for the pow-wow. On this trip, I drove that beautiful 1964 Corvette Sting Ray my wife won at the Black Bear Casino last year. We finally got it running good again. This was my first long trip in that classic American sports car. The day was hot and sunny. I took the top down and cruised south on the freeway; the exhaust rumbled behind me. The sun tanned my skin darker except where I was wearing a headband. I now have a Corvette stripe across the middle of my forehead. I was playing music tapes from the sixties; had to, I guess.

The dance was just good, met some new friends, saw some old friends. I heard real old music there. Pat saw some berries near where we were camping and couldn't resist picking some. We ate the berries in our oatmeal one morning. My wife was dancing jingle, and I was giving rides in that Corvette. Some people were having their picture taken while sitting behind the steering wheel. Others wanted to see the engine. The folks seemed to like the Fond du Lac license plates that say Rez Car.

I cruised the interstate on the way home, exhaust still rumbling behind me. I was singing to the music. I drove the speed limit, and a lot of people were passing me. I let them, knew I could go faster than almost anything that came along. I waved at other Corvette drivers as I rumbled home.

With my family, I made a trip to Morton, Minnesota, to take part in a memorial ceremony for Pfc. Norman E. Dow. He was my wife's uncle and had died during World War II in France. He was a member of the 51st Armored Infantry Battalion, 4th Armored Division. He had made the landing at Normandy, was wounded, and continued fighting until he was mortally wounded, on December 1, 1944. His family never received the medals he had won. Lucy Taylor Jacobs helped in the search to find the medals and was successful, so we had the memorial ceremony.

The doings were held in a large tent near the Morton Community Center. It looked like more than a hundred people gathered to take part. The ceremony was done by Al Kitto. Everything started with a pipe ceremony, then singing of certain songs followed. Roland Chulu Columbus gave a eulogy, which was followed by an honor song. The VFW honor guard from Redwood Falls took part in the honoring of Norman Dow. Ray Earley, US Marine Corps Vietnam vet, and I talked about what it was like to come back from the war since Pfc. Dow didn't return from his war. Ray talked about how PTSD affects combat veterans. I recited a few poems. Ray and I raised Norman Dow's American flag and then dropped it down to half mast. The medals, two Purple Hearts, a Bronze Star, and theater ribbons, were presented to Pfc. Dow's sister Carol Taylor. We all lined up and shook her hand. The veterans there were given star quilt blankets, more singing went on, and we ate together. I was honored to take part in this memorial service. It is good to see how the people from Morton honored their veterans.

Question: How much did your 401(k) lose in value?
Answer: The same as my 401(a), (b), (c), (d), (e), (f), (g), (h), (i), and (j)—nothing.

We have been manoominke (making wild rice) here. *National Geographic Today* sent a writer and cameraman here to record how we do it. I don't know when it will be aired, and it isn't important because we don't have cable or satellite TV. What was important was some people learned how and why we make wild rice every year.

Fond du Lac Follies motored to Michigan. No, didn't take the Corvette. The other car has cruise control and air. When I was coming through Chicago, I was doing seventy-five and cars were passing me on both sides. I drove tactical. I was going to see Megan (Aerol) Noori and her new baby, Fionna, who just got here seven weeks ago. I taught that baby the stick-out-her-tongue trick. She learned right away how to do it. I smiled. Asmat and Shannon were there, then gone to their schools. On the way home, I stopped in Indiana. My nephew lives there. My sister Jean was getting ready to drive back to Sawyer. We convoyed for a while until we got split up by traffic or a casino. I got home. The Corvette was waiting.

Fond du Lac Follies jetted to California. I was invited to Fullerton College in Fullerton to recite poetry and talk about writing to the students. I took a little plane from Duluth to Chicago. In Chicago, I had to walk about a mile to get to the gate where I boarded the big jet for California. I had a window seat, and I watched America unfolding beneath the wings. First, I was seeing farm fields, then the earth started to look wrinkly. We were at thirty-seven thousand feet and I couldn't make out too many details. I liked the way the rivers just went anywhere they wanted. I began to see snow as we flew over Colorado. I saw the snowcapped peaks of the Rocky Mountains. Then we flew over the brown deserts of Nevada, and the pilot pointed out Hoover Dam to the passengers. I began to see the rounded mountains of California.

When we landed at John Wayne Airport I got suspicious. The whole area looked like a bank of fog. It wasn't fog; it was smog. I asked my host about the air. He said the smog used to be much worse. The air looks pretty worse to me, I thought. I couldn't see the details of buildings that were two blocks away. The air smelled like the ocean, sort of fishy. I will say right now that I don't trust air that I can see. I knew I had to breathe that thick air for three days. The thought of returning to the cool Minnesota air made it bearable.

I had a good time talking with the students and staff of the college. The evening reading had two guitar players and a poet named Susan Sink. More than four hundred people showed up to hear my words. I even met a couple of skins who told me they appreciated the way I ask questions in my monthly newspaper column, The Fond du Lac Follies. I always meet skins.

Once again it was airplane time. I was watching the under-the-wing show in reverse, first rounded mountains, then the Rockies, then it was getting dark so all I saw were the lights of America. When I got to Duluth, I went outside and breathed deeply of that good Minnesota air. I felt sorry for those people in California who were breathing thick air.

For Veterans Day, Fond du Lac Follies motored to the Lac Court Oreilles (LCO) Rez to hang out with veterans. I traveled with Vietnam vet Ray Earley, USMC, (United States Marine Corps, also known as Uncle Sam's Misguided Children). It was the last official ride in that pretty Corvette for the year. We looked good, two old vets in a Vette. Paul Demain, the editor of *News from Indian Country*, invited me down to sign books at the local trading post. Vern Martin asked me to say some words at the gathering of veterans at the tribal headquarters when I was at LCO. I met some old friends and made some new ones. We offered tobacco for the fire, flinched when they did a rifle salute. It felt good to be among veterans on our day.

Blood quantum. That is a problem we are facing as Indian people. The Reservation people here at Fond du Lac will be discussing that vexing problem soon. The Reservation Business Committee is sending a questionnaire asking for input. The first question is: what do you think that the standard for membership in the Minnesota Chippewa Tribe (MCT) or the Fond du Lac Band should be?

A) Retain the current standard (one-fourth degree MCT blood quantum)
B) Retain a degree blood quantum requirement, but include non-MCT blood
C) Reduce the blood quantum requirement to one-eighth MCT blood
D) Reduce the blood quantum requirement to one-eighth, including non-MCT blood
E) Adopt a standard for membership by descendancy: if one of your parents are enrolled, you are eligible.

All of this talk about blood quantum reminds me of my only blood quantum story. When I first heard about blood quantum, I was in the first grade at Pipestone, the federal boarding school. I was labeled as fifteen-sixteenths Minnesota Chippewa Indian. I didn't know which one of my sixteenths was something else. Later on, when I graduated from Carlton High School, in '61, I was checking on scholarships and found that I was thirteen-sixteenths Minnesota Chippewa Indian. Hmmm . . . And the last time I checked, I was eleven-sixteenths. I have quit checking because I am losing my blood somewhere. Where did my blood go? Was it those trips to the blood bank? The mosquitoes? I am ever so careful about nosebleeds and shaving. All I know is there is not enough blood for my grandchildren to be enrolled.

Chapter 2

Bundles Is One Year Young—2003

At this point in mid-December I don't know which is coming quicker, Christmas or a war against Iraq (the sequel). Both are foolish ideas to my way of thinking. Peace on earth? Get real. I know one young Marine officer who is prepared to do his duty and will place his life in danger. That lieutenant is from this Rez. I am already mourning the people who will get hurt or die in the upcoming war. I shall grieve for their families as I grieve for America. I don't want to hear war stories, especially new war stories. I have heard enough from the old war stories to know it is always bad. Tell me again why we are going to be killing people in the name of peace?

What happened to the war on terror? My television gives me many images, and the two I remember most are bomb-laden jet planes launching from an aircraft carrier and President George Bush walking and waving at the crowd, always waving. I've got an idea. Remember all the American flags we saw after 9/11? We can save them and put them on the aluminum caskets that will be coming home.

When I was growing up, there were lean times, and I sometimes went hungry. Now I can go to the casino buffet and eat very well for very little money. I was one of the first employees when gambling came to this Rez. I was unemployed at the time and gambling gave me a job. My sons went to work building and staffing the casinos. On this Rez, we have never had an outside management firm. We take care of our own affairs. There were some small mistakes made along the way, but people have learned, and that is why I am proud to say our casino managers are from this Reservation.

Fond du Lac Follies motored waabanong (to the east) to Onigamiinsing (Duluth) to hear one of my favorite Anishinaabeg poets. Marcie Rendon appeared at the agindaasoowigamigong (library) located right on Superior Street in the downtown area. Marcie's words are so concise, and I really like her delivery. When she started, she told a funny story about her car catching fire. When the fire was out, a civilian asked her what she was going to do. She looked up and saw a fingernail place, and Marcie said she was going to get nails done.

The anaamisag Ozhaawashko-Abiwin (basement green room) was crowded; the chairs were filled and it was standing room for the folks who came to hear her and her ikidowinan (words). What a nice way to spend an evening. The event was called Native Words and was presented by the Friends of the St. Paul Public Library, Birchbark Books, Black Bear Crossings, the Duluth Public Library, Minnesota Historical Society Press, and SASE, The Write Place. The same group had earlier sponsored a reading by Native authors at Black Bear Crossings at the Como Pavilion.

Question: Why are the Rez politicians' signs still up six
months after the election?
Answer: Because there is another election coming in
three and a half years.

Dibaajimoyaang biboong, winter is the time for telling stories, so we did that in Sawyer. The Reservation
Business Committee (RBC)was asked to provide mileage and lodging for the storytellers. They readily agreed.
Jean Dufault, the director of the Sawyer Center, took
over the planning. At fifteen minutes before the scheduled feast, there were about ten people standing around
waiting. The preparation for the feast actually started
the night before, when our resident French chef, Francois (What? You don't have a French chef?), started
cooking the moose meat. He cooked it all night long,
braising it with his secret sauces. Francois also cooked
some soup and fried the walleye. Community members
brought their favorite dishes for the feast. People started
to trickle in and the trickle became a flood. The elders
lined up first to get their food. The line of people standing behind them stretched out the door. The people were
eating moose meat, deer meat, wild rice, Pat Northrup's
fry bread, and dishes prepared by members of the community. The moose meat was tender and tasty. As the
people gathered to eat, they were talking and laughing,
visiting and eating. It felt good to be among that crowd
of people. One person reported that it was good to gather

in that old center without a body lying at the front of the room. The old Sawyer Center was the scene of many funerals over the years. After the meal, the people moved to the new center, where the storytelling was going to be held. Vic Swan brought his drum to open the doings. Sitting with him were Zac Earley, Virgil Sohm, and Jim Northrup III. The song and drum drew everyone together. RBC member Butch Martineau welcomed the crowd and said what a good idea it was to have the storytelling in Sawyer. Bryan Jon Maciewski acted as the MC. He introduced Rick Gresczyk, who brought six students and a teacher from the Four Winds School in Minneapolis. The Four Winds students, Leah Blakely, Anthony Conners, Ashley Conners, Thorne LaPointe, Wakiya LaPoint, and Justin Richards, introduced themselves in their languages. Their teacher, Pam Anderson, was smiling with pride as she listened to the students. Rick told a few stories and said how important it was to learn and use the language. I recited a few poems and told a few stories. There were more than two hundred people who came to hear the stories. That showed me the power of stories and storytellers. It also showed me the people are thirsting for the oral tradition of storytelling.

Marcie Rendon came up to the microphone and began weaving her words to the appreciative audience. I think she made some new fans. It is always good to hear her poems.

Heid Erdrich, who was selling books from a table set up for Birchbark Books, was up next, and she recited a few poems and read stories. We like Heid in Sawyer. She also brought her new baby to the doings.

Al Hunter was then given the microphone, and he

wowed us with his words. Al and Bryon Jon did a few things together. Bryon played his guitar to accompany Al's words. Bryon played his guitar and used his harmonica to entertain the crowd. I found myself singing along with him as he strummed and sang. Vic Swan ended the evening with two songs. People were asking when we were going to do such an event again. One woman came from Madison, Wisconsin. I saw others from Nett Lake and the Fond du Lac Tribal and Community College. Right now, we are looking ahead to the next full moon time for another storytelling event.

Fond du Lac Follies jetted to Phoenix, Arizona, for a veteran's symposium at the Ak-Chin Resort and Casino. My friend from my Marine Corps days came to visit from near Gallup, New Mexico. Ted Charles and I were together when we were in the 1st Marine Corps Regiment at Camp Pendleton, California, in the early '60s. Ted and I took a ride and looked at the desert plants. I learned about saguaro cactus. It takes ten years to grow one inch, a hundred years for the first branch. We took pictures and told stories. Ted and I motored to Sacaton, Arizona, to see the Ira Hayes Memorial. We both had grown up hearing about this Pima Marine who had helped raise the flag on Iwo Jima, where "uncommon valor was a common virtue."

Another friend who came to visit was Sara Begay. She writes for the *Navajo Times* and thought there was a story in Ted and I getting together. While I was there, I had a chance to visit Maricopa High School. I talked to the students about writing and storytelling. They told me they had never heard of an Indian writer. After a few days, it was time to put my long johns on for the return to Minnesota.

My grandson Ezigaa and godson, Zac, have been setting snares. Don't tell the animal rights people, but they came home with three frozen bunnies. We ate rabbit soup. We are living up to our tribal nickname of "rabbit chokers" here on this Rez.

I have a new son. He used to be my grandson, but now he is my son. Pat and I have adopted Aaron Ezigaa Howard Dow Northrup. Judge Dale Wolf of Carlton County held the hearing for the adoption. One funny part of the proceedings was when our lawyer asked us questions. One question she asked was if Aaron had a biological father. We thought he did because there has been only one Immaculate Conception so far. The judge laughed at the question, as did the court clerk.

Aaron has been living at this house on Northrup Road most of his life, all twelve years. It seems like just last week he was just a little bundle of baby. He gurgled little baby noises and smelled baby powdery. He spent hours in my arms as I showed him the world.

Then he was a toddler; we picked agates together as we walked the trail of life. We spent much time in the woods, looking for bark, berries, and good memories.

That boy now knows about maple trees, birch trees, and wild rice. Little by little, he has been learning how to be an Anishinaabe on the Rez.

He can introduce himself in Ojibwemowin and hears the language spoken every day. Ezigaa is looking for the day when he is taller than his dad. Now he is almost a teenager and comes complete with baggy pants, hair on his lip, and cellyphone on his hip. Imagine, that little bundle of baby now has his own phone number.

Aaron's brother, Mato, said, "I know you'll be my uncle, but will you still be my brudder, too?" Hey, we're still making Fonjalackers here in Fond du Lac.

It was just yesterday when I wrote about turning fifty years old. It has actually been ten years since that event. Now that I am almost sixty, I have some more thoughts on life and death, living and dying. First of all, I am glad to be here. I have attended many funerals since I was fifty. It is almost getting to the point where I know more dead people than living ones. I am more concerned about my health at this end of my life. When I was young, I used to think I was indestructible. The aches, pains, and groans have slowly convinced me otherwise. I feel strong, but just not so long. I am blessed, never thought I would make it past the Vietnam War.

We were waiting the arrival of my newest grandson. Jim and Lisa went to St. Mary's Hospital in Duluth where

Shabub was born. He was slightly overdue in arriving. I fully expected the baby to come walking out. Jim said not only walking, but also whistling and asking for the car keys. The baby arrived after some labor and he is beautiful. His black hair is long and shiny. Now is that twelve or thirteen grandchildren? It is hard to get a count when they keep moving around so much.

The sap is dripping; it is the beginning of sugar bush. I am ready; I have taps, jugs, buckets, a couple of boiling kettles, and firewood. Now all I need is cool nights and warm days. I saw an eagle flying around when I was checking the test tree in the yard. I tap a couple of trees here to see what the trees are doing in the sugar bush. I wonder who will visit this year? Once again, I am happy to take part in the seasonal cycles of the Anishinaabe. I smile when I see my children and grandchildren taking part also. I can almost picture them telling their grand-children about life with the seasons.

How can I write about mundane matters like sugar bush when a war is happening in Iraq? How can I blithely talk about my children and grandchildren when others are targets for American munitions? I have to; otherwise I would go crazy looking at the craziness out there. By the time I write the next Follies, we will know more than we know now. I grieve for America.

I like living in the quiet village of Sawyer. The

sound of the wind in the trees is soothing. Our sugar bush went well this year. I like living the seasons of the Anishinaabe. It feels right to be doing what my parents and grandparents did at this time of the year. It felt good to be sitting outside in the warm spring sun.

We boiled sap in the yard again this year. The fire in the pit, the glowing coals under the cast iron kettle felt as good as the sun. The heat from the fire went deep into my body. It was like my skin warmed up first, then I began to feel the heat inside; bones, ligaments, and organs were all being heated by that fire. I felt the warmth of the fire long after I walked away. This year we used bacon instead of balsam branches to keep the sap from boiling over. It worked. The sap would begin to foam up and threaten to boil over. The sap touched the bacon and went back down. The laughs and stories heard while sitting around the fire were good. We had visitors from two college classes, a few civilians. We make three different kinds of treats here: syrup, sugar cakes, and sugar. We are maple rich here in Sawyer. Miigwech.

The war in Iraq is mostly over, but I don't think the troops will be coming home anytime soon. There are still countries over there that have oil. According to the news media, there is one Marine still missing in action. He is in my prayers. I haven't heard of any weapons of mass destruction being found in Iraq. I thought that is why the United States invaded Iraq. I am grieving for my country still.

Corvette. Here is some of what I spent on parts and insurance so far: niizhwaak niizhtana ashi bezhig waabik (passenger side window), niizhwaak nanimidana ashi niiwin waabik (insurance), niizhwaak waabik (U joints), niizhwaak waabik (ignition), ingodwaasimidana ashi ingodwaaswi waabik (rear wheel bearings), nisimidana ashi niizh waabik (cover), nimidana ashi niizh waabik (another cover), ishwaasimidana ashi niswi waabik (module), niimidana ashi niizh waabik (spark plug wires), niishtana ashi biizhig waabik (headlights). The cost of gasoline isn't included here.

Question: How do you say "culture vulture" in Ojibberish?
Answer: Anishaa-wannabe.

In a recent casino story, I was the victim of a crime. My wife, Pat, and I went to play an evening of bingo at the Black Bear. On the way to the bingo hall, I played a slot machine. That last white seven fell into place and I won two hundred quarters. I got a cup for the coins, and we went to the bingo hall. While paying for my bingo package, I set the cup on the counter. I then picked up my bingo stuff and went to find a place to sit. I found a good spot and spread my bingo stuff around the table. Then, I remembered the cup of quarters. Pat went to look for it, but it wasn't where I left it. She told security about it, and they went to work. They played the bingo hall videotape and found out who picked up the cup of coins. Two security people walked in to the hall and spoke to a man. He got up, left his wife sitting there, and went out of the bingo hall with security. Every time the bingo hall doors would open, I could see the man's wife looking up to see if it was her husband coming back.

A short while later, a security man came up and told me I had a choice. I could sign a complaint and the man would go to jail; they would also keep my quarters as evidence. The second choice was the casino could kick the man out for a period of time and would give me my money back right away. I chose the way that would get the man kicked out for making me a victim of a crime.

Overall, I was impressed with the way casino security handled the matter. They identified the culprit and got me my money back. So, if you are dumb enough to leave your money lying around, do it at the Black Bear Casino because they can help. I won at bingo, too.

Fond du Lac Follies motored to Bayfield, Wisconsin, for an art fair. It was a two-day event. Charlie Nahganub rode with me to the doings on the first day. Of course, I drove the Corvette along the southern shore of Lake Superior. The sun was warm; the sky was blue except where the white puffy clouds were sailing along. Janis Joplin was singing to us as we cruised down the two-lane highway that had curves, hills, and dales and no traffic. During some parts of the ride I could smell sweetgrass in the air. I liked the many shades of green shown by the trees. I liked the wind blowing through my hair. Red headband or not, my hair looked like Don King's at the end of the ride.

In Bayfield, I did what I would be doing at home and that is to work with birch bark. The art fair was held in the pavilion downtown. My shaded table was twenty feet from Lake Superior and there was a nice breeze. I sewed and answered questions about what I was doing. One part that left me wondering was when people would say, "I bet they didn't have clothespins to hold the bark together two hundred years ago." I would ask them why they expected me to live as Anishinaabeg did two hundred years ago. I would further ask them if they came to Bayfield with a horse and buggy, or did they arrive in a car.

Charlie and I motored home along Highway 13. It was just getting dark, and we were weaving in and out of the deer. I counted twenty-one deer in a sixty-mile stretch. I went alone to the art fair the second day. It was another great Corvette day. Once again, I sewed on birch bark and answered questions.

I met a lot of old friends and made some new ones. I looked up, and a man wearing blue coveralls was walking toward me. I learned he was John Herrington, the astronaut, the first American Indian in space. He is Chickasaw and was born in Oklahoma.

John Herrington walked around the room to talk to the artists. He spent time with each one and shook hands with them. When he was done with the artists, he gave a short talk, living up to his role as a role model.

When he was finished, I asked him if he wanted to go for a ride in the Corvette. He said yes, and we cruised down Highway 13 together. After a couple of miles, I asked him if he wanted to drive. I figured if the government trusted him with a space shuttle, I could trust him with the Corvette. He laughed out loud when he felt the power of that machine. He said it was almost as fast as his shuttle. After the ride, I packed up for the trip home. Once again, I was weaving through the deer, only counted fifteen of them this time.

The president of the United States told us repeatedly that Saddam Hussein has weapons of mass destruction. That is why it was necessary to invade and drive him out of the seat of power. Now some sixty days after the hostilities are over, Americans are dying there at the rate of one a day. It is with great sadness that I learned that more Americans have died in this war than in the previous Gulf War. I am worried about the never-ending war on terror. My son Ezigaa is now thirteen, and in a few short years he will be eighteen, the same age I was when I joined the United States Marine Corps. Wouldn't it be ironic if we moved to Vietnam to keep him safe? Jean-Paul Sartre said, "When the rich make war, it's the poor that die."

Corvette news: Ingodwaak naanimidana daswaabik (starter).

You gotta be able to walk through eagle moo (droppings) if you want to be an eagle feather hunter. I was reminded of that fact recently. My son Matthew brought home an eagle feather and told me he knew where some eagles lived. We motored off the Rez in an unnamed direction to an unnamed lake. It was Minnesota-nice weather with scattered showers. We went where it wasn't scattering.

At the lake we used the public landing. My son launched his boat, the *Jackie Lee*, with practiced ease. Matthew got the boat and trailer last year from a guy who had to suddenly leave town. But that is a whole other story that has nothing to do with eagle feathers. The *Jackie Lee* just needed a platform so it could be used for spearing as sanctioned by the 1837 and 1854 treaties.

We putt-putted west from the landing. Right away, I noticed an island in the lake. It was easy to notice because the front of the boat was pointing right at it. I saw a bird flying circles around the island. Matthew said this was one of the younger eagles because it was still brown all over. I noted the familiar wing movements of the young eagle.

We landed at the island, got out, and stretched our sea legs. I showed my son my method for hunting eagle feathers. First, I offered some tobacco. I used a stick to sweep the low bushes aside. I could then see all the way to the ground. That action also let the mosquitoes and deer-flies know that we were there, ready to pay our blood dues.

The first one we found was a white piece of eagle fluff, the kind that young girls like to wear in their hair at powwows. My son found a solid white tail feather. It was like the feathers got larger the more we found. I spotted a dark one, the kind you see on some guys' hats.

The last one we found was a wing feather, easily as long as a box of commodity cheese. Matthew and I thanked everyone responsible for giving us the seven eagle feathers we brought home. We also made good father/son memories that day.

———————————————————

Question: Why'd you go to boarding school at age six?
Answer: It was either that or marry the girl.

———————————————————

One of the joys in my life is having grandchildren. Bundles came to visit. I don't know what his birth certificate name is. He is one year young. His dad, Tony, brought him here to Northrup Road complete with diapers, wipes, bottles, and formula mix. Bundles looked afraid of me when he first came because he hadn't seen me for a while. After I made goofy faces and smiled a lot at him, he warmed up and was soon smiling back. He has a few baby tricks; one of them is rubbing his finger past his lips and making a bub, bub, bub sound. We spent a lot of time on the floor, crawling around looking at stuff. Everything is all so new to him. When I am crawling with the baby, I don't feel any of my sixty years. Bundles, come visit again, daga.

———————————————————

Ezigaa and I went ricing. It was his first time on Perch Lake as a ricer; we could call it a rite of passage for this young Anishinaabe boy. I am proud of my thirteen-year-old son. I remembered back to when I was his age, when I went ricing for the first time.

We loaded up the pickup with the tools we would need. The aluminum canoe was first, then the tamarack pole with the diamond willow fork. I gave him my cedar knockers to use. I checked and made sure we had water and a lunch. I also brought a paddle.

The day was sunny with a slight wind from the west. At the rice landing, I could see other ricers already in the lake ready to begin ricing. It smelled like lake there. The lake looked like the lyrical amber waves of grain. I saw how the wind had leaned the rice in one direction.

I told Ezigaa how I was going to zigzag into the wind until I got to the other side of the lake. I also told him how I wanted to hear the knockers saying shush-shush, shush-shush, shush-shush, and not shush . . . shush . . . shush.

It just felt right to be doing what we were doing. We offered tobacco in gratitude. I saw a V of geese and ducks flying into the wind. I also noticed there were a lot more ricers than there used to be five years ago. Maybe because the Rez was buying rice at the landing for four bucks a pound?

I could hear the sound of his rice knockers hitting the rice, also the sound of the rice hitting the inside of the canoe. We could hear other ricers laughing and talking. When we got to the western end of the lake, I turned the canoe around and headed east. It was easy poling with the wind. Ezigaa was knocking on both sides of the canoe. I looked at the rice he had harvested. The bottom of the canoe was covered and the rice was bearding up, looked like a porcupine quilt.

I told my son we could take a break whenever he wanted. I didn't want this to seem like hard work. I called the first break; actually, that day I called all of the breaks, except when he called one because he was hungry.

We ate our lunch while sitting in the middle of the rice. I showed my boy how I like to strip rice with my fingers while just sitting there. At one point in our travels around the lake, I got hung up on a mud flat. My boy learned how hard it is to pole a canoe in a mudflat.

We finished the day on the lake and were satisfied with the amount of rice we had gathered. We rode home and spread the rice out on a tarp so it could dry. Ezigaa removed the debris from the rice as I got the fire ready. I built the fire in the pit in the yard. I rolled the huge cast iron kettle over to the fire and propped it up at an angle.

My son brought a basket of rice to the kettle and put it inside. I began stirring and flipping the rice as it parched. The wood fire smelled just fine, as did the smell of parching rice. The rice made a swishing sound as I parched it, keeping it moving in the kettle. After the rice was parched, we put it away and got ready for the second day of the harvest.

We went to Dead Fish Lake, where one of my grandfathers was raised. I felt connected to the old ways, old days. It was almost like my grampa was watching and approving of what we were doing on the lake. An eagle flew over in anticlockwise circles. He was flying low enough so we could see his white head and white tail. We had a better second day of ricing. My boy knocked twice as much rice as he did the first day. He said he was getting the hang of it. I could hear the pride in his voice. We brought the rice home, where we dried it in the sun for a little while. Once again we used the black cast iron kettle to parch the rice. We then danced on it, rubbing the rice to grind the hulls off. We usually have to dance and fan the rice three times. I like watching the color change from the brown of the hulls to the green of the rice. We cleaned the rice by taking out the grains that still had the hulls on after the dancing and fanning. Ezigaa is now a ricer.

Fond du Lac is passing gas out to those who have signed up with the Fond du Lac Propane Company. According to Mary Durfee, the company has more than four hundred customers on the Rez. What a progressive thought, I thought. The Rez bought the supplies, trucks, tanks, and hired three permanent employees, and now my house is warmed with Fonjalack gas. I eagerly signed up when I found out the cost was quite a bit lower than the off-Rez propane suppliers. I think the Rez made a good decision to enter the propane gas business. I will be warm this winter with Fonjalack gas.

Someone decided that I have way too much money, so I was given a 1964 Corvette. All I have to do is keep it on the road. I drove that car everywhere for many months this summer. Kak and I even used it when we were gathering birch bark. But for the last month or so, the car has been a very expensive lawn ornament. A valve slipped and went through one of the pistons.

The motor then chewed itself up. My son Matthew was driving at the time and he felt awful, vowing to never drive the car again. Ray Earley and I proceeded to take the engine apart. I was apprehensive about diving into such a complicated project. We began by taking off the parts that would get in the way of pulling the motor out. The hood, the fan, and the alternator all came off pretty easy. The troubles began when we were actually lifting the motor out. A bolt got stuck, and as we lifted it snapped and broke off a large piece of the transmission housing.

So, there I was with a blown engine and a broken transmission. We took the engine apart and found out what went wrong. We found pieces of one piston in the oil pan. Ouch. I heard that Buck Savage had some crate motors, so I bought one from him. We took the good parts off the old engine and put them on the new one. Ray went to the Cities and bought a used transmission, and I thought we were almost on the road again. I am no longer afraid of my car because I have taken it apart and put it back together. I hope to drive that pretty car at least once before the snow falls.

Fond du Lac Follies motored to meet kick-ass writer Adrian Louis. Adrian is a skin from the Lovelock Paiute Tribe. He has taught in the English Department at Southwest State University in Marshall, Minnesota, since 1999. His best known work is *Skins*, a novel made into a movie starring Graham Greene and Eric Schweig. I know it is well known because I can find it at the video rental section of the Sawyer store. Adrian has also written twelve books of poetry.

It was an easy road trip, just pointed the truck toward Nebraska, but stopped when we got to Marshall. There was one gambling interlude at Prairies Edge Casino before we got to Marshall. We broke even and that is good because I can use the money. We visited and exchanged gifts. For the doings, I recited poetry and shared a few questions from the Fond du Lac Follies with the audience. Afterward, Adrian arranged for a cheese and wine kind-of-social in a local bar. We had a good time telling stories and lies. I told him, when I grow up I want to write as well as he does.

Zhaawanong. To the south went the Fond du Lac Follies. Road trip. My son Matthew, horseshoe partner Pea, and I went to Little Rock, Arkansas. We made the trip there and back in the silver Silverado. The Corvette is hibernating. Of course, we did a map recon before we left. Looked like about a thousand miles. As the man said, "The journey of a thousand miles begins with a single throwing of your butt up on the truck seats."

When we arrived, Matthew noticed that the people in Arkansas looked like the people back home. We did notice one difference, however. The people in the South walked slower than we did. It seemed like they spoke slower, too. The people we met were friendly.

After getting settled in, we began meeting other skins. Kim Blaeser (White Earth) was there as was Patty Loew (Bad River). Selene Phillips (Flambeau) was also a presenter. Paul Demain, his wife, and child were also part of the mix. There were other skins there from the Southwest, but the Shinnobs from up North had them outnumbered.

Kim Blaeser asked if I would help with her play she was presenting. She also asked Matthew to read. The play was about two strong women and a jiibay (spirit) and their struggle to establish a museum on the Reservation by outwitting the corrupt tribal leader.

We all came together to take part in the Third Annual Sequoyah Research Center Symposium at the University of Arkansas at Little Rock. Dr. Dan Littlefield welcomed us. Dan has been archiving American Indian newspapers for more than ten years.

My part as a presenter was to read prose and recite poetry. After I did my reading, we rehearsed Kim's play. Patty Loew and Kim played the sisters. Selene Phillips was the jiibay, Matthew played a writer, and I played the corrupt tribal politician.

That evening we performed *Shinnob Jep* in downtown Little Rock at the Arkansas Museum. The play went well. Matthew played the part of John Johnson Jr. Kim was Tradish Ikwe for the evening. Pea was Franklin Lake, and I was Al Treebark. We laughed our way through it, as did the audience. The audience began laughing with the first answer and continued all the way through until the end. After the 1,066-mile trip home, I had a severe case of truck ass.

Chapter 3

Moose Alert on Northrup Road—2004

Question: Why don't you hear more of the Ojibwe language spoken?

Answer: Because people don't know that *Zhaaganaashiimong* means the "English language," *I'iw ina* means "Is that so?" and *Eya, geget gosha* means "Yes, for sure."

I got a pleasant surprise the other night. My youngest son, Aaron, brought home some eighth-grade homework. He had a textbook, 1,032 pages long, called *Literature: Timeless Voices, Timeless Themes* by Prentice Hall. He was going to read a story for class. I told him I would read the story, and we could talk about it when we were finished. Instead of turning to the assigned page, he opened it to page 845. There I saw my name and a title of a poem I had written about my brother, Rod Northrup. It is called "Wahbegan." My boy had a smile on his face when he showed me my work. It is thrilling to know my alma mater, Carlton High School, is using my words to teach my son literature. I think my boy is dad proud.

Fond du Lac Follies motored to Grand Marais, Minnesota. The Friends of the Library wanted me to come up and tell stories. My wife, Patricia, and I took turns driving. She had the freeway parts, and I had the two-lane parts. We were talking while driving up Highway 61. It was mostly about Aaron, the thirteen-year-old who is the center of our lives. He doesn't need a babysitter anymore. Yup, hair on his lip, cellyphone on his hip. Ezigaa, as we call him, is living life with the seasons with us, that boy. In the spring we spear fish and make maple syrup. I also take the Corvette out of storage. In the summer we make birch bark fanning baskets, and I drive to powwows in the Corvette. In the fall we make wild rice and hunt, and I put the Corvette back in storage. In the winter, I write stories, we snare rabbits, and I order parts for the Corvette.

The reading was done in the Johnson Heritage log cabin outfit downtown. I began by introducing myself in Ojibwe. It seemed like the proper thing to do. It was a good reading, standing room only except for those who were sitting on the floor. There musta been seventy-five people who came to hear stories on that wintry evening. I told Luke Warmwater stories, asked a few questions from the Follies, and recited war poetry because this country is at war. I told stories for an hour and a half, and it was good.

Question: What's wrong with him?
Answer: While in a blackout, he drove into a whiteout.

My cousin Rathide stopped by for a visit the other day. We sat at the kitchen table, drank coffee, gossiped about this one and that one. We played cribbage in the sunshine as we got into some serious visiting. As old men do, we began to compare medical maladies. Rathide said he went to Duluth and a guy cut him with a knife. Rathide sat back on his haunches and told me what happened. He said he had a pain in his behind. A pain in my injii-diish, thought it was a hemi, him said. He then told of his visit to the clinic, where the nurse thought he had a hemi, too. She gave him some antibiotics, pain pills, stool softener, and a cream to use on the affected area.

Rathide went home and looked ahead to taking care of his behind. It was hard to sit until his son gave him a foam donut. After a couple of days, the tender area became swollen and most painful. He walked funny back to the clinic, and the nurse arranged for emergency surgery. She said the surgeon was waiting for him in the emergency room. He was told to undress and was given half a robe. The surgeon examined him and told him he had an abscess. The cutting doctor explained that they had to cut into the lump and drain it. The gas doctor said they were giving him oxygen to help him relax. Rathide woke up an hour and a half later in the recovery room. As he was coming around, he heard the sound of a woman moaning in pain. She was in the next bed and had a clutch of nurses around her. She was morphined and the moans turned into snores. Rathide stayed in the recovery room until he recovered and then left the hospital.

The pain in his nether region was gone, but now he

had dual exhausts in his rump. The wound was about an inch away from the regular channel. The wound was left open so it could heal from the bottom out. A strip of medicated gauze was packed into the wound. The recovery at home was long and painful. The torture was scheduled for two times a day for ten days. It took three people to change the dressing and pack the wound. One nurse to hold the cheeks open, one nurse to hold the wound open as the main torturer packed gauze past the lips of the wound.

"All they got out of me was my name, rank, and serial number. Oh yeah, some bloody gauze, too," he said, as he shifted in his chair. I poured more coffee and tried not to picture the picture Rathide painted. Rathide said he went back to the doctor after a couple three days of torture. The doctor examined him and said the wound was healing. He didn't need the gauze torture anymore. We continued playing cribbage quietly because I couldn't top his story.

Fond du Lac Follies motored to Saint Paul to talk with the state senators. I haven't seen those guys since the Treaty Rights Fight of '88. The senators were considering a resolution for the revitalization of the Dakota and Ojibwe languages in Minnesota. I was invited to tell stories about boarding school in Hearing Room 123, State Capitol building, the one with the golden horses. The senators sat at their long table; each one of the five had a microphone. The witnesses sat at a smaller table sharing a single microphone. I told the senators about a six-year-old boy feeling the pain of wanting to be home. I recited my poem "Ditched." I told the senators how area farmers were paid a bounty for reporting runaways. I told the senators . . . gego zazaagiziken. Then I shut up. I heard later that the resolution passed.

The Iraq war came to Cloquet, Minnesota. Tuddy Angell's son, Levi, was killed in Iraq when his Humvee was hit by an RPG, a rocket-propelled grenade. My family and I went to the church for the visitation. I studied the family photos before I walked up to the casket. Levi was wearing his dress blues with a Purple Heart. I saluted the young Marine. I shook hands with Tuddy, and our eyes met. A young girl, a relative of the Marine, began crying. Once we got outside, I offered tobacco.

It is Corvette weather. Me and that beautiful machine are rumbling around the highways of northern Minnesota. This time—niizosagoonswaabik, that was all it took to get it back on the road again. That '64 Sting Ray is sure expensive to keep on the road. I forget about all that when I push down on the gas pedal. Ezigaa and I go for a cruise around the lake when he comes home from school. We ride until he reminds me he has homework to do. Nitaawis Deano Bishop has a Corvette. We are thinking of forming the Fond du Lac Corvette Club. Two club members in the club. No dues, no benefits except for the thrill of rumbling around the roads of Minnesota. Hey, we could take turns being president of the club?

There was a moose alert here on Northrup Road. My sister Nita called me and told me how a moose walked close by her house and was headed my way. Nita lives about five hundred yards south of me, so we sounded the Moose Alert. We had company visiting from the Lower Sioux Reservation. There were five kids playing in the yard, and it didn't take them long to come running up to the deck. The six adults visiting inside quickly ran out to join the kids on the deck. There were twenty-two eyeballs looking for the moose. We waited and watched. Nothing, no moose. A later report said the moose took a turn and walked near where Bill Moose used to live. Of course, that started everyone telling moose and other animal stories. Pat told about the three bears that walked through our yard. It was a mother and two cubs. The kids came running in to tell us they saw bears coming. The three bears walked by the house looking like they owned it.

I told of the time I was walking in the woods north of Big Lake between the road and the pipeline. I was looking for birch bark. I saw movement and froze in place. A large brown critter came strolling into view. I went through my checklist . . . dog, no . . . wolf, no . . . coyote, no . . . bobcat, no . . . puma, yes. I was looking at a cougar. We were about fifty yards apart. The big cat looked at me. I looked back. About then I realized I was no longer the top dog in the food chain. It made me wish I had more than a Buck knife. I wanted a gun, a machine gun, grenades, or artillery, maybe even close air support. The big cat and I had a staring contest that lasted several hours, but was really only about sixty seconds. I admired the beautiful cat. It looked graceful while just standing there. The only movement was the occasional flick of his long tail. I remember thinking it wouldn't be a good idea to get into a footrace against those claws and teeth. The brownish-yellow puma turned his head, and I saw his muscles rippling as he glided away. I think it was a him, could have been a her. I didn't want to get close enough to find out. The last thing I saw was that long tail waving good-bye.

Pat and I motored east to visit with some Seneca people at Salamanca, New York. The skins were celebrating their tribal library's twenty-fifth anniversary. I was invited to come and say a few words to the celebrants. We took turns driving. The directions were simple . . . hang a left at Chicago. We motored down the turnpikes and tollways of America. I could see the green Allegheny Mountains. We set up camp in the Holiday Inn Express in Salamanca.

The high point of the visit was seeing Warren Skye Sr. That eighty-year-old man was moving around like he was forty years younger. He taught me one Seneca word when I shared a gig with him in Brockport, New York, a few years back. The feast with the library celebrants contained the traditional corn, beans, and squash. There were quite a few suit-and-tie Seneca there.

We motored west on the interstate and then the Ohio Turnpike. At one of those rest areas, we stopped for a break, a stretch, Starbucks coffee, and a smoke.

Pat and I were standing on the grass off the sidewalk as Americans walked by in all directions.

One American woman looked at us and began walking toward us. As she walked closer, she pointed at my chest and asked loudly, "What are those?" I knew she was pointing at the bear claw necklace I usually wear.

I acted like she was talking about my shirt, so I said, "This? It is a T-shirt. A lot of people are wearing them nowadays."

"I'd like to buy them from you," she said as she reached into my space to feel the claws. I gave her a little smile and told her she couldn't buy them.

Later, as Pat and I got back on the turnpike, we talked about bold Americans. That is when I came up with the answer to the woman's final question about buying my claws. I should have said, "Lady, you don't have enough money to buy these claws."

I was a day late and a retort short.

We have reached a significant milestone here on Northrup Road. My son Aaron, fourteen winters, took a small step to becoming a man. The milestone is (drum roll, please) Aaron brought home his first paycheck. This is the first time he ever paid a FICA tax. I took him to the Sawyer Store, where he carefully signed his name on the back of the check. Sara counted out the money. His eyes were smiling as the twenties piled up in his hand. He folded the money in half and stuck it in his right front pocket. It wasn't too many winters ago when he was learning how to walk, riding in a car seat. We were riding out to the sugar bush, and he was looking for eagles. I remember him scampering around on top of the snow while we were breaking through. This year we will rice again. He is my ricing partner. I started poling when I was his age, so I think he will be standing up in front of the canoe this year.

When Aaron saw his ma at home, he said mom and threw the wad of money in the air. The twenties fluttered down and they both laughed. They gathered up the moolah and headed to town. That boy, becoming a man, wanted a new cellyphone. I wonder if he will call me from his end of the canoe? Mii sa iw.

Fond du Lac Follies jetted to New York City for the doings at Lincoln Center. The doings is called *La Casita*. I think that is a Spanish word, but it wasn't on any of my commods labels so I didn't learn it. I think I will be in town the same time the Republicans are having their convention. I shall keep much distance between myself and those folks. I met Cochise Anderson at the Minneapolis airport. We went through the security screening, where I removed my moccasins and sent them through the X-ray machine. When I got on the airplane, I realized my name was not on the no-fly list. It is good to know I am not a threat to this nation's security.

Cochise and I landed at Newark, where we caught a shuttle to our hotel, at 96th and Broadway. It was a tiny, tiny room we shared. Smokers had to rake their filthy, smelly, expensive habit outside, I learned.

La Casita at Lincoln Center was great. I learned that Cochise and I were joining a troupe of performers.

Musicians and poets took turns on the stage and did what we do. We did two performances at Lincoln Center, one at the Langston Hughes Library in Queens, and one at the Point, a community center in the Bronx. The audiences liked our work, and I got to hang out with the other performers. One of my favorites was a group from California called Conjunto Hueyapan, a Mexican harp and string ensemble. Their music had me tapping my foot just hard.

I walked with the protesters at the Republican Convention for just a short time. There sure were a lot of police around. I saw four layers of helicopters over Manhattan. That was way too much city for me, and I was glad to get on the plane and get back to Sawyer. When I got home, I raised my arms in thanksgiving and just breathed deeply while looking at all of the green of the woods.

Fond du Lac Follies also jetted to Washington, DC, to take part in a historic event. It was the grand opening of the National Museum of the American Indian. Now I will be able to tell my great-grandchildren that I was there when they opened the doors. My wife, Pat, and I reported in to the airport. We checked a bag and were issued boarding passes. We went through the security screening and began to wait. We waited a long time for that airplane. We heard the jet make a pass at the runway before we were informed the plane wasn't going to land because of the fog in Duluth.

We showed up again the next morning and went through the airplane boarding process. It was a short flight to Minneapolis, where we connected with the next airplane. We began to see Indian faces sprinkled in the crowd. We deplaned at Reagan National Airport and got in line for a taxi. Fifteen bucks later and we were at our hotel, the Holiday Inn Capital, just three blocks from the NMAI building. We became Holiday Inndians for the duration of the visit. The lobby was just full of Indians checking in.

After we set up camp in the hotel room, we went out to explore, looking for the museum. We walked just a couple of blocks before we saw the building. It looked like a big brownish-yellow pile of rocks compared to the other buildings near the Mall. I later learned the stone on the outside of the building came from Minnesota. I didn't see any corners in that building. There were Indians walking toward the building and some walking away. I put on my Indian-smiling-at-another-Indian face and kept it on the whole time we were in D and C. It felt good to be a part of something so big.

The museum was still closed, but we walked around the outside just looking. I saw some people going through a side door. I wandered over and got in line. After going through the metal detector, I found out my name wasn't on the list. I told them I thought my name was supposed to be on the list. The list checker checked again and couldn't find me. She said, "We'll just pencil you in . . . your wife, too." We were issued a folder that told us we were attending a symposium on indigenous museums around the world. Also inside the folder I found a ticket for a preview showing of the museum and a ticket for the reception later that day.

We walked around the Mall surrounded by a sea of Indian faces; we were smiling just hard at each other. Using our preview tickets, we began to tour the museum. I was glad to see George Morrison featured so prominently. I noted that the Fond du Lac Tribal and Community College loaned one of their Morrison art pieces to the museum. We only saw the top two floors of the museum before we had to leave. There was just too much stuff to look at. While walking on the Mall, we met Sara Begay and Keevin Lewis, our old friends who work in the radio part of the Smithsonian. There were Indian faces everywhere.

We marched in the procession. I think they were going in alphabetical order by height. We were late and missed marching with the Minnesota Chippewa, so we became Oneida for the duration of the procession. It was said there were 25,000 Indians marching. I only counted 24,892. I wondered what the legal limit for Indians was. I thought they were going to pull the whole Mall over for having too many Indians in one place.

The highlight of my trip east was meeting Alex and Amelia Lewis. They are old family friends I have known since 1962. It was good to see them again and share a few memories.

I wish I had a nickel for every camera I saw. I would have enough nickels to keno twenty-four hours straight if I could depend on my Depends.

Later that year, Fond du Lac Follies traveled to Waashtanong (Washington, DC) to do a reading at the NMAI. I was honored to be asked to do this. My son Matthew volunteered to come along as my bodyguard/

driver. His life partner, Jackie, came along, too. She played the part of the attack chick. Ray Earley also wanted to travel to DC because it would be the Marine Corps's birthday while we were there, also Veterans Day.

We decided to drive rather than fly. Matthew got a rental SUV and we packed it full of the clothes we would need for the five-day trip. We went through the blue and red states until we got to Michigan. In Ann Arbor we stopped to visit with Megan Noori. She fed us lasagna as we visited. Megan shared some of her translations with me. I am glad there are people in other places who are preserving the language by using it.

We slept like we were clubbed after that long ride from Minnesota. Ray and I went to the Vietnam Veterans Memorial to pay our respects to all of those dead Americans from the war. We saw a lot of Vietnam vets there. It felt good to be among so many living Marines.

After we left the wall, Ray and I got into a limo that was to take us to Virginia. I read to the employees of Freddie Mac, the mortgage outfit. It was American Indian month, and I was their contribution to diversity. I told Rez stories for a while, and then we ate buffalo burgers with the employees.

On November 10, 2004, we celebrated the Marine Corps's birthday at the wall. There were a lot more Marines there. I saw a Marine Corps general walking toward us. He looked sharp in his dress blues. When he saw Ray and me standing at the edge of the crowd, he came over to greet us. He took off one white glove to shake our hands. I was thrilled because generals usually don't hang around with snuffies like us.

Lt. General McCorkle was wearing aviator wings

and a Purple Heart on his uniform. The general was traveling with Col. Butler, a helicopter pilot from our war. Later, we heard the commandant's birthday message read and ate a piece of Marine Corps birthday cake. True to tradition, the oldest and youngest Marine present cut the cake with a sword. The Marines lined up to eat the cake. A homeless-appearing man joined the line. He came through the line three times to eat cake.

That evening, we went to the NMAI, where I was scheduled to read. My entourage, son Matthew, daughter Heather, pal Jackie, sidekick Ray, and friend Colette, followed me to the green room that was mostly orange. Suzan Shown Harjo was the hostess for the evening. I read a while then joined Ms. Harjo at the table, where I took questions from the audience members. I read again, and it was good.

The next morning we were happy to head back to Minnesota. There were too many sirens, helicopters, and trains in that Waashtanong. We only stopped to take on and discharge liquids as we motored across the blue and red states. Mii sa iw.

Chapter 4

Enough for a Shinnob, Not Enough for a Chimook—2005

The Corvette is hibernating. I won't drive it for at least ninety days. In the meantime, I am buying parts that I will put on it as soon as it warms up a little.

I bask in the warmth of living with an extended family here in this little village of Sawyer. I have brothers and sisters, aunties and uncles living close by. I see at least one cousin every time I go to the store or the casino. And, we always have a grandchild or two visiting.

The current visitor is called Bundles, sometimes Buns, but very rarely Bunny. He is all of three feet high and takes the stairs one foot at a time. He can feed himself with a spoon; I noticed that this morning when we were eating our oatmeal together. He carries a stuffed dog for security and lets me hold it occasionally.

He was acting kind of whiny one evening. I suppose he missed being home. I told him to bring his dog over and lie down on the couch next to me. He did and was asleep within two minutes. I carried him to his bed. He slept, still clutching his stuffed dog named Doggie. One morning he surprised me when he walked over and turned on the television. My house is full of the music of Sesame Street, Barney, Teletubbies, and Mr. Rogers every day.

Bundles is on the verge of talking, so I am teaching him some Ojibwe words. He says "boozhoo" when greeting someone. He has trouble with "giga-waabamin," however. When I say "zoogipoon" and point at the falling snow, he says "boon." He says "boogid" especially clear. Won't it be funny when he returns to his Ho Chunk and Dakota parents and speaks Ojibwe to them?

My son Joe brings his son Joe and daughter Sarice to visit every couple of days. Sarice is just beginning the crawling stage of her life. She has large, expressive eyes and when my sister Nancy saw them, she said that little girl could see everything. Today the grandchildren will play with each other. What joy the young ones bring to this extended family. I am blessed.

I have been trying to avoid writing about the war in Iraq, but it is impossible. As a former grunt in the Vietnam War, I am very interested in what happens to the troops there. The question still remains from the first Gulf War: how can we support the troops without encouraging the war makers? I don't remember ever pledging allegiance to Halliburton, George Bush, Donald Rumsfeld, or Karl Rove. The reasons given for starting the war were bogus, the intelligence was flawed, and good people are dying almost daily. America . . . are you ready for the veterans to come home from this war?

Biboon, it is winter here in northern Minnesota. When

I step outside in the early morning, I see the stars. They seem closer and brighter somehow. The dark pines sending their full-moon black shadows across the white snow look good to my eyes. I appreciate the gift of another morning. It was easy to feel close to the Creator.

Nimbiindaakoojige. I see we have had more snow overnight. It outlines the branches of the pines. There is a rounded shape to everything. The sky is dark, getting lighter to the east. And it is quiet. The snow is as deep as a car fender. We did have one night when it was thirty below zero, but because we have been through winters before, our vehicles started because we prepared them.

During the day when the wind picks up a bit, I can see the snow blowing off the branches. It comes down in shimmering sheets of snow. The falling curtains remind me of the waves that pulse through, the jiibayag niimi'idiwag (northern lights).

Of course, here on Northrup Road, we are prepared for winter. There are a lot of Northrups here. My first cousin, Geraldine Defoe née Northrup, lives at the north end. Then there is my house, then my son Joe's house right across the road from my son Matthew's house. Behind Joe is my sister Nancy, who lives next door to my sister Suzy, who is next door to my sister Nita, who is right next to my brother Vern.

There are a few other Northrups scattered around Sawyer. My brothers Russ and Jeff live here, as does my sister Jean and son Jim. We are trying to come up with a name for this part of Sawyer. So far we have selected and rejected Northrup Flats, Northrup Heights, Northrupolis, Northrup Estates, Northrupville. We are open for any suggestions.

Ziinzibaakwadwaapine. That is the Ojibwe word for *diabetes*, and I have been diagnosed as having the disease. In my studies, I learned that as an Anishinaabe I am more likely to get high blood-sugar readings than any other population group. Also, as a Vietnam veteran who was exposed to Agent Orange, I am likely to get the disease. I am a twofer, got two reasons to get the disease. How am I fighting the disease? Under the excellent care of the Mino-ayaawin Clinic here on the Rez, I think I am doing fine. I have been issued blood-testing equipment and every morning I monitor my blood sugar level. There is a slight hesitation as I poke myself each time for that little drop of blood. I take prescribed drugs to help keep the blood sugar low.

It was an abnormal beginning on our trip to Normal. I had been invited to that central Illinois town to tell stories for the Native American Student Association. The doings were held at Illinois State University. My son Matthew volunteered to drive; Jackie came along because she hadn't ever seen Normal. It was snowing when we left Sawyer in the silver Silverado. We were headed south on the High Bridge in Duluth. A gust of wind and a stretch of black ice sent us sliding sideways. It is not fun to slide sideways at forty-five miles an hour. Matthew was spinning the steering wheel and tap dancing on the pedals; first we slide one way, then the other way.

I had plenty of time to think during the slides. I remember thinking we would begin to play bumper cars, and I would never see Normal ever. I pictured the truck going over the guardrail and into the water sixty feet below. Someone in the front seat was saying, "Oh moo, oh moo, oh moo," only they were saying it in English.

Time slows down when you are in a sideways slide. I had time to look out the back window to see cars and trucks coming behind us. Gradually, the slides got smaller as Matthew regained control of the truck. It was quiet for a while, then pretty soon we all began talking fast about the slide on the bridge. We relived the skid for a hundred miles, at least.

It took us nine hours to get near Normal. We found our motel and set up camp. The next morning we went to Bone Auditorium. I think it was named after someone named Bone. We told stories all day. At first, the crowd size was small (I don't know if three people counts as a crowd). But during the later sessions, more people came to hear stories. We ate good. The second day of marathon storytelling commenced. The audience was a group of third-, fourth-, and fifth-grade Normal children. Once again we ate good.

As soon as the last session was done, we got in the truck and pointed it north. The almost full moon followed us across the flatlands of Illinois, Iowa, and Minnesota. We arrived in Sawyer in the middle of the night. I got out of the truck. The cold air, the sound of the crunchy snow told me I was home. I had enough of Normal.

Fond du Lac Follies motored (I don't like to fly anymore) to Whitewater, Wisconsin, to take part in the Third Annual UW–Whitewater Native Pride Week. I was invited to come and tell Vietnam War stories. The speakers and their topics were as follows: Ada Deer, educator and the former head of the BIA, was going to talk about "Influential Native American Women." Neil Hall from Canada was going to speak about "The Truth about the Creation of Man." The self-proclaimed Cherokee Ward Churchill was coming to speak about "Racism against the American Indian."

We knew the self-proclaimed Cherokee was scheduled to speak at 7:00 PM, so we drove to the scene. I knew we were getting close because we began seeing protest signs. Police and satellite TV trucks surrounded the Hamilton Center. There was a group of about fifty protesters holding signs. One sign read "Don't steal my identity." I had a ticket for the event, but the police wouldn't let me in the building. Their security checkpoint was taken down and the building was sealed.

What a disappointment. I wanted to meet this self-proclaimed Cherokee. Instead, we went back to the motel and talked about culture vultures and wannabes in general and this self-proclaimed Cherokee in particular. He reminded me of that old joke: We got a Cherokee princess in our family, but we don't talk about him. We also talked about his claimed combat experience as a paratrooper, a long-range reconnaissance patrol member who walked point. Records show that he was trained as a public information specialist. Musta been a combat movie projector operator, we surmised.

I gave my talk the following night. I didn't see one police officer or one satellite TV truck. Instead, it was an auditorium filled with people who wanted to see and hear from a real skin who actually walked point in

Vietnam. I did recite one poem called "Walking Point." Ray and I laughed about that self-proclaimed Cherokee all the way home. We did make one stop to eat at a casino. We laughed again because that casino was very friendly to us.

Winter was winding down and spring was blooming in. It was time to think about spring things. We make maple sugar every year because my grampa made maple syrup every year. And like my grampa, I move my sugar bush around. One year I was by Peno's Bay on Big Lake; another year I was behind the Catholic cemetery. This year it was the Ditchbanks.

My son Aaron and I motored to the Ditchbanks area of the Rez to look at the sugar bush we had used before. The snow was knee-deep. I almost wished I had brought the snowshoes along. We looked at the prospective sugar bush. It was quiet. Aaron and I used a game trail to walk through the woods while looking at the maple trees. The trail had deer tracks with wolf tracks on top of them. Aaron and I made up a story to go along with the tracks. It felt good to be outside after a long winter in.

I am looking forward to making birch bark fanning baskets.

We have had another milestone in our family history. My wife, Patricia Ann Northrup, graduated from the

Fond du Lac Tribal and Community College, in Cloquet. It all began several years ago when she got her GED. She took classes in business, finance, ethics, Ojibwe, English, and speech. I was proud as she came marching out to get her diploma. She wore the yellow sash that identified her as a member of Phi Beta Kappa. I especially like her reasons for going. She once told me she wanted to be a positive role model for her grandchildren. I thought that was the best reason she could have given. Aaron, my too-cool fifteen-year-old son, was with me applauding as Pat was recognized for her work. We basked in reflected glory.

On the way home, I decided to wear Pat's mortarboard. The yellow tassel and the medicine wheel eagle feather swayed back and forth as I was driving. About halfway home I asked Aaron if he wanted to wear her hat for a while. He said no, he will just wait a couple of years and wear his own mortarboard. Pat's role model part seems to be working already.

The following day we had a brief ceremony to thank the spirits for helping Pat reach her goal. Lee Staples came and smoked his pipe. We put out a food dish for the spirits.

Pat is now looking forward to her next degree.

It is that time of the year again. I have been cruising through the woods using the treaty rights reserved by my ancestors. In the 1837 and 1854 treaties, the Anishinaabeg reserved the right to hunt, fish, and gather in the ceded territories. I am using the 1964 Corvette my wife won at the casino to gather birch bark. I have discovered I can fit twelve large sheets of bark in that beautiful machine. The sheets fold nicely over the convertible top. When I close the trunk lid, it looks like any other shiny, gray, '64 Corvette Sting Ray in northern Minnesota.

When I am out gathering bark, I also gather basswood bark and green willow. These are the other two parts we need for the baskets we make. *Nooshkaachinaagan* is the Ojibwe word for a winnowing basket. They are made during the summer and used in the fall by the Anishinaabeg people to winnow wild rice. The basket is made using three gifts of the Creator. The body of the basket is wiigwaas (birch). The frame is made from green willow, oziisigobimizh. The frame is sewn to the birch using the inner bark of the basswood tree, wiigob.

I bring the materials home to this little HUD house we call NITTS, the Northrup Institute of Traditional Technology in Sawyer. Here we assemble the baskets. The birch is prepared for use. The corners are located and cut. The birch is folded into a basket shape and the corners are sewn. A piece of bark is added at each end. The willow sticks are peeled, two are tied together, nose to tail, using willow bark. The sticks are fitted to the birch bark. Using the sticks as a guide, a line is drawn around the perimeter of the basket. A rough cut is made. Two pieces of bark are added to the sides. The sticks are tied together and a final cut is made. The sticks are then sewn to the top of the basket. We use a mookomaan (knife), moozhwaagan (scissors), and migoos (awl) to make the basket. The basket will last forty years if it is not treated like plastic or aluminum. Then it is biodegradable, like us.

Fond du Lac Follies motored in that beautiful Corvette to the contest powwow at Hinkles. While walking around, we met many people we know, including Clyde Bellecourt. That AIMster guy told me a funny story. It seems an elder was brought in to show students how to make black ash baskets. At the end of the day the black ash log was pungent, and it was decided to store the log outside. It was placed in a PVC pipe and covered with a plastic trash bag. The janitor discovered the bag. He called the cops, who called Homeland Security, who called the bomb squad. The bag was blown up, scattering plastic bits all around. The log was undamaged in the blast. The moral of the story was: Don't mess with the feds; they'll blow your black ash up.

Fond du Lac Follies motored and motored to Montana. We headed west on Highway 210 until we got to Walker, Minnesota, where we made a small donation at the Northern Lights Casino. We continued west. Pat and I were headed for Great Falls, Montana, to visit an American Indian symposium. His name was American Indian Nations: Yesterday, Today, and Tomorrow.

It seemed like Montana had more sky than North Dakota. The land was mostly rock and sage; didn't see any plastic bags of civilization blowing around.

After our part of the symposium was over, we motored north to drive Highway 2 back to Minnesota. We knew it went by the Palace Casino in Cass Lake.

Just as it was getting dark, a small critter ran across the road. The raccoon made it, but then he decided to go back across. Hay, esibaniban. When we got back to Sawyer, I got out of the truck and looked at the trees. I looked at them a long time before the mosquitoes told me to go inside.

Question: How do you say "No hotdogs"?
Answer: Gaawiin-ers.

Fond du Lac Follies motored again to Washington, DC, to visit the Smithsonian's National Museum of the American Indian. This time we were invited to demonstrate how we make birch bark baskets. Patricia and I loaded the silver Silverado with tools and materials for making baskets and headed east. We were treated very well by the museum people. We set up our basket-making operation in the main rotunda. The doors of the museum were opened, and people came by to see what we were doing. The tourists came from many different countries, including the United States. The second day of demonstrating went well also. Pat and I explained what we were doing to the many visitors. The questions were intelligent, and people walked away with some new information. It was a delight working there.

The third day went well, too, but toward the end of the day our visit was marred by a white man with neck of red. With a sneer on his lip and in his voice, he told me Indians didn't have clothespins two hundred years ago (we use them to hold the bark pieces together). What did they use then? I told him they used common sense, a split stick, or a temporary stitch. While he was digesting that, I asked him if he came to the museum by car or horse and buggy. He said a car brought him. Then I asked him why he expected me to live two hundred years ago and he got to evolve. He didn't answer, but then complimented me on how well I use the English language. I thanked him and told him it came in handy because I am also an author, playwright, poet, and columnist. His neck turned redder, and he quickly walked away. The other tourists were laughing at him as he was leaving. I've seen his type before. All in all, it was a good trip to Washington, DC. I would go back again if they asked.

We have a visitor here at the World Headquarters of the Fond du Lac Follies. Her name is Ramona, and she is from Rome, where she attends La Sapienta University. She is writing her master's thesis on the Anishinaabe and gambling. We are field research. Ramona was detained by Homeland Security when she arrived in Detroit. She missed her connecting flights and rode into town on the Greyhound bus. The next morning, Ramona and I motored to Red Lake for the parade and powwow. An aspiring princess perched on the Corvette for the ride down the parade route. Deborah Goodwin smiled and waved at the crowd. Her younger sister, Audrey, threw out candy to the spectators. Ramona and I Corvetted back to Sawyer, where Patricia had supper waiting. So, in the interests of international scholarship, we took Ramona to bingo.

Once again we were given the gift of wild rice. My son Aaron and I built a canoe rack for the back of the silver Silverado. We used scraps of lumber we had around the house. The rack building went well except for that one two-by-four leg. I cut it three times and it was still too short. My son Jim and I chose Perch Lake because we like that rice. Fifty years ago, I stood at that same landing and watched my parents and grandparents make rice on that lake. Jim and I made an offering of tobacco together. There was a nice breeze, the rice bending nicely. The sun was warm but not hot.

On the south shore I could see one bright red maple tree. I could hear people laughing. Maybe they were laughing about the Shinnobs who went ricing at the wrong time. There were dark clouds approaching, lightning and thunder sounds, and flashes in the sky. The Shinnobs paddled into the storm. There was a flash of orange light near the aluminum canoe. They returned to shore; ricing was over for the day. A Sawyer Shinnob said they were trying to knock rice and parch it at the same time.

We brought our gift from the lake to the ricing camp set up in the yard. My nephew Kris and I cleaned the rice. We used our birch bark baskets while removing the leaves, stalks, and lily pads from the rice. I showed Kris how I like to build a parching fire. He rolled the black cast iron kettle to the fire. We lifted it into place. We both offered tobacco. Kris parched the rice, learning on the job. I showed him the J-stroke I use when flipping the rice. By the third batch, Kris was feeling good about his parching. Jeez, I am making another ricer. After many years in America, Kris is coming home.

Ramona from Roma is enjoying her studies of the Anishinaabe while staying here at the World Headquarters of the Fond du Lac Follies. The phone rings, and after I say boozhoo I hear a lot of Italian words, and I know the phone call is for Ramona. She and her mother talk at least once a day. One time I thought I heard boozhoo with an Italian accent when I answered the phone. Ramona spends a lot of time on her computer. She is learning quite a few Ojibwe words also. Ramona is scheduled to rejoin her family in Italy in a few weeks. We shall miss her, will miss my house smelling like Italian cooking. Ramona went back to Rome after her three-month visit here I'd like to think we learned from each other while she was here. Her breakfast habit of pouring dry cereal in her coffee was kind of strange, about as strange as bacon grease on oatmeal, I guess. She left a bicycle here. I will find out if she wants me to mail it to her. Our trails will cross again.

The Iraq war drags on. American men and women are dying daily. I have heard *Iraq* is Arabic for "Vietnam."

More and more people are beginning to believe we were lied into a war. I am one of those people.

———————————————————

My sister Nancy June Krieg died as a result of injuries from a house fire. She fought death for a month before she died. She leaves a husband, Richard, and two sons, Kris and Robert, numerous brothers and sisters, even more numerous nieces and nephews and so many friends. She was forty-eight years old. Lee Staples conducted the traditional ceremonies. My son Jim kept the fire burning outside the old Sawyer Center for four days. The family and community members came together to visit, tell Nancy June stories, and eat a feast. I shall miss you for a long time, Nancy June.

Chapter 5

Just Make Everyone
Four-Fourths—2006

Niminwendam biboon omaa noongom. Winter is here
and I like it. We just had a foot of snow fall, and I like
the way it softens things up. It sure is quiet. The snow
sticks to the pine trees around the yard. The wind comes
up and the snow falls to the ground in clumps and in
shimmering curtains. I am glad I picked up my tools
before the snow came, otherwise I wouldn't see them
until spring. The snowplow drivers like it. They finally
have something to push around. My sister Nancy June's
husband has a little tractor with a plow, and he enjoys
moving the snow. He keeps my driveway clear.

In the mornings the sun comes up and paints the
clouds many colors. I especially like the days when
we have purple turning to red to yellow. Once again
the quiet soothes me. In the evening during the time
of the full moon, I like looking at the shadows of the
trees on the snow. When I was young, I remember my
mother, Alice, using a crosscut saw to cut firewood. She
was working outside to keep her babies warm inside.
We have come a long way since then. Now, thanks to
the Rez propane company, all I have to do is turn the
thermostat up if I feel a chill. The Sawyer Community

Center gave my son Aaron Ezigaa a season pass for the Mont du Lac ski hill. He will be enjoying winter in his own way.

Question: What do you call those who come back from relocation, schools, and jobs away from the Rez?
Answer: Returnabes.

I attended a review hearing with Ray Earley about his son Zac's enrollment in the Minnesota Chippewa Tribe. The doings were done in the basement of the new Tribal Headquarters south of Cass Lake. The building looked snazzy. Sure enough, there were tribal rolls at the tribal rolls meeting, coffee, too. The panel said they would further review the matter for ninety days. They would continue checking their documents to verify Zac's blood quantum. Ray said he would continue with his research, looking for that missing one-one hundred twenty-eighth. Bill Houle, a former Fond du Lac Rez chairman, told me his solution to the BQ problem. We have the right to define our members. Just make everyone four-fourths again. We could do it every ten years. I thought that idea would be a gift to our grandchildren. We have to do something before we breed ourselves out of existence.

Looking through reports at a recent RBC meeting, I learned the Reservation spent $46,498.55 on the Ojibwe language program last year. I wondered where the money went, because at the Ojibwe language table we have been asking for Ojibwe language materials for several years and have yet to see anything.

I got up to speak about how the Ojibwe language at the Black Bear Casino was forbidden. I mentioned how a friend of mine was warned about using Ojibwe on the radio. All he said was, "Niwii zagaswaa" (I want to smoke.) A supervisor talked to him about using the language like that in that setting.

The chairman reassured me the RBC position was to always promote the use of the Ojibwe, not hinder it.

My grandson, the one I call Bimose, stops by every morning when he has school. He walks to the school bus stop with my son Ezigaa. We sit at the kitchen table and talk about things important to this five-year-old kindergarten student. He tells me what he does in school or how his kitten got out and spent the night outside. We always manage to do some counting in Ojibwe. That boy can count to twenty now and before long will be able to count to thirty, forty, and even fifty. I wonder if he will remember counting with his grampa when he is thirty, forty, or even fifty?

Yes, we are making maple syrup on the Fond du Lac Reservation. My brother Russ is tapping on the west side of Sawyer, my uncle Larry Shabiash is tapping trees in his usual place on the west side of Big Lake. My son Jim is tapping trees out in the Ditchbanks. Mike Murray is by Peno's Bay tapping. Bruce Savage is making syrup to sell, so I guess he is tapping everywhere he can.

I went to the quiet woods with my sons Joe and Ezigaa and grandson James W. Northrup IV. We call him Niiwin because he is the fourth Jim Northrup. The sky was bright blue, the sun was quite warm as we waded through the knee-deep snow. It was like walking upstairs. The first tree I tapped was wet, and the sap came through the tap pulsing like a heartbeat.

My wife, Pat, and I carried our powwow chairs along to the woods because we are now old people. I was glad to see my crew knew the difference between oak and maple trees. Pat and I sat in the warm sun as the boys went from tree to tree. They had a nice little system going; Joe drilled the trees, Ezigaa cleaned the hole of shavings and tapped the tap into the tree, Niiwin hung a milk jug on the tap. I watched and smiled, proud as I saw my young ones learning.

We went home to wait for the trees to do their part. At the sugar camp in the yard, we built a small fire so we could dig a hole for the big fire. We placed the kettle over the hole. We were ready to begin boiling the sap into syrup.

We did it. We made maple syrup again. Nitaawichige. This is one of my favoritest seasonal activities. I feel connected with the old ways, old days of the Anishinaabe, when I make syrup. I grew up watching my grampa making maple syrup every year. When I was away from home, I would get sugar cakes in the mail. I ate the sugar cakes when I was in that federal boarding school at Pipestone, Minnesota. I ate the sugar cakes in An Hoa, South Vietnam. The taste always brought me home.

When outside, I like the cool wind and warm sun. Except for the crows, it is quiet in the woods. We can hear the train going by in downtown Sawyer. The train horn at the crossings sounding like a Johnny Cash song.

My crew this year consisted of my son Joe, son Ezigaa, grandsons Bimose and Niiwin, and friend Kak. Joe was the oldest at 26, Bimose was six. We had other helpers drift in and out. Joe and Kak, Ezigaa and grandson Niiwin drilled and carved taps. Our goal was to put two hundred taps in the trees. In the woods the snow was knee-deep. We just made trails from tree to tree. Pat took pictures of our sugar bush process. On her rez, in southern Minnesota, they have maple trees, but no one has tapped them for a long time. My wife was going to show her friends and family how we make syrup here. We drilled and tapped at a new sugar bush this year.

After a couple of days of checking, we didn't like it anymore, so we moved to another reliable spot. Some trees just don't run. The crew and I used buckets and barrels to gather the sap from the hanging jugs. Bimose was issued a bucket and a warning about spilling sap. He watched his dad do a couple of trees before he tried one.

At home we prepared to boil sap. Earlier, Ezigaa and Niiwin had built a fire to thaw the ground so we could dig a fire pit. I smiled when I saw they had made a platform of balsam branches to keep the fire dry. I showed the boys that trick about ten years ago. I also saw how they wove the birch bark strips through the dry wood. I was glad my son Jim had delivered firewood for our boilings. We dug the pit and laid the fire. We rolled the old cast iron kettle to the fire. The big black kettle is just called kettle. We wiped the kettle clean and suspended it with chains from the frame.

We begin to make syrup. The kettle is filled with filtered sap and we begin a long day. We set up powwow chairs around the fire pit. The heat of the fire reaches everyone. The clear sap begins to boil. A line of bubbles begins to form at the edge of the kettle. The steam comes off slowly at first, then faster as the sap heats up. Pretty soon there is a rolling boil going on. I hang a strip of bacon over the foam to keep it from boiling over. The hot sap comes up, touches the bacon, and goes back down. It is automatic.

Joe and I build a wall of firewood to keep the heat under the kettle. We just stand the wood on the ground and lean it into the kettle. We add sap to the kettle until we don't have anymore. By this time the sap is brown colored. At just the right time, we take it off the fire and bring the hot sap into the house. Pat filters and boils the sap some more. The house smells like the inside of a maple tree.

When it has boiled down enough, she filters it again and again. She pours the hot syrup into pint and quart jars. The rows of brown jars on the kitchen table make me feel like a rich man. I know what I'll be putting on my oatmeal every morning. Joe and Kak are talking about their own sugar bush next year. They know what has to be done.

Bimose had a lot of ammo for show-and-tell at school. This was Ezigaa's sixteenth consecutive year making syrup. I am glad we used tobacco throughout the season. I smiled because I knew my grampa would be proud of me.

Fond du Lac Follies motored to the Black Bear Casino for the white-guy ceremony called Turning of the Earth. This groundbreaking of the $100 million casino/hotel upgrade had already been rescheduled because of the heavy rain. This time they decided to hold the doings under the front entrance canopy. A front-end loader from Fond du Lac's construction company was used to deliver a load of masonry sand to the driveway. A cart full of gold shovels was also pushed into place.

A crowd of about a hundred people milled around the front entrance. I even saw some Fonjalackers in the milling crowd. The Cedar Creek drum group was also standing by. Executive director Mike Himango did a masterful job as master of ceremonies. He spoke of his long association with gambling here at Fond du Lac. Mike spoke of the early days, when bingo first started. He even told the crowd that I was one of the first bingo callers. I responded by saying, "Under the O, 69."

Mike introduced nitaawis Rick Defoe, who saged the sand pile, lit his pipe, and spoke in Ojibwe. I smiled because I could understand a lot of the Ojibwe Rick was using. He translated into English what he said during his blessing. The Cedar Creek Singers then sang an honor song. They sounded good, and I like the look on Kak's face when he reaches upstairs for those high notes.

The Walsh Bishop members spoke briefly about the project. The MC also introduced the construction firm members from Kraus Anderson. They also spoke briefly, and I was thankful because I was looking forward to the feast. My stomach was growling louder than the semi-trucks jake-breaking down the nearby off-ramp of I-35.

Everyone that spoke was then issued a gold shovel, and they lined up next to the pile of sand. The Turning of the Earth Ceremony was on. Each one stuck their shovel in the sand and flipped some in the air. The photographers were ready and cameras flashed. The photographers asked the dignitaries to do it again. They ended up flipping the sand three times. I was impressed with the Turning of the Earth Ceremony.

After that, the crowd began milling around again. There were happy smiles all about, also much hand-shaking. Butch Martineau came through the crowd still holding his gold shovel. He smiled and gave me the shovel. I looked closely at the shovel. First of all, it wasn't a gold shovel; it was just painted a gold color. Second, I noticed the shovel was made in China. What a treasure, I thought. Someone went through a lot of trouble to get that shovel all the way from China to me. The Rez was giving out presents, too. Mine was a pen set that included a little flashlight and a tire gauge. This came from China, too. I quickly drove home and gathered my children and grandchildren around to look at and admire my golden shovel and pen, light, and tire gauge. They oohed and aahed.

My brother Jeff Northrup died. He was forty-three. For those from large extended families, you know what comes next. We had a four-day ceremonial fire. We had ceremonies and sad feelings. We will miss you Jeff, giga-waabamin miinawaa.

The Thirteenth Annual Fond du Lac Veterans Powwow was held in Sawyer. Why do we number these things? What makes them so different that they need a numerical designation? Is it now traditional? I like the way this Reservation honors the veterans.

We set up our shelter and I proudly hung my Marine Corps flag. Pat danced while I sewed birch. The shade and water began attracting people. It seemed like everyone who came by had a little story to tell. One woman talked about her mom's triple, no quadruple, bypass surgery. Another vented about tribal enrollment and blood quantum. Still another talked about his prostate cancer. One guy came by and talked for quite a while. He was a soft-spoken guy, so I really couldn't hear what he was saying. It didn't matter since I had my listening face on. When he was done he just walked away. I wondered if there was a sign that said Listening Booth near our shelter. I sat in the shade and sewed baskets. It was a hot powwow, meaning the weather. At one point I did see an eagle fly over the doings on the shores of Big Lake, again. The Rez was generous with their gifts for the veterans. I got a pound of rice, an insulated cup, a new hooded jacket, and a hat that says Fond du Lac Veteran and Ogichidaa. I met old friends, made some new friends, and met some I didn't want to be my friends. That would include the two teenage girls who began a fistfight in front of our shelter.

As a student of the Ojibwe language, I always smile when I see the language used in public places. The Reservation's C-store is a good example. In bold letters it says, Nagaajiwaanong Adaawewigamig, identifying the place by using the Ojibwe words for this Reservation and what happens in the store. While motoring around the Rez, I found another example. On the back of the Reservation's white septic tank truck, the Honey Bucket, as it is sometimes called, I read an Ojibwe word. It is written in dust just above the main drain. It simply says Moo with an arrow pointing to the outlet valve.

Fond du Lac Follies motored to the Black Bear Casino/ Hotel/Golf Course for the Third Annual Veterans Golf Tournament. I don't really give a care about golf, but my son Joseph was on Mike Peacock's team for the event. Pat and I went down there to be cheerleaders for our son.

When we got there, we swapped the Silverado for a golf cart. We followed Joe to the driving range, where we watched him hit a bucket of balls to warm up for the tournament. He even let us hit a couple of balls. We both hit grass cutters, worm burners. Instead of soaring through the air, our balls followed the nap of the earth and rolled to a stop just fifty feet from the tee. That is when I remembered that I didn't golf and also remembered why. We had fun in that golf cart, following the cart trail. I was wishing I was driving the Corvette on that narrow strip of curvy blacktop. All in all, we saw eleven birdies, three eagles, and one fat porcupine. Gaag was just waddling across the fairway. That score was good enough to earn Mike's team third place and a cash prize.

Question: Aaniishwiin maanendamoyan noongom?
Answer: Gii-zhoomiingweni niwiiw gii-gashkigwaadang nimakasinan.
Question: What is worrying you now?
Answer: My wife was smiling as she was sewing my moccasins.

Fond du Lac Follies motored to Milwaukee at the invitation of Kim Blaeser to help promote the new book she edited. It is called *Traces in Blood, Bone, and Stone: Contemporary Ojibwe Poetry,* published by Loonfeather Press. Inside are contributions from thirty-two Ojibwe poets. The event was called The Voice of the Crane: A Celebration of Ojibwe Literature and was held at the University of Wisconsin at Milwaukee. I met Kim and the assembled poets at a nice place just off the campus of UW–M. There I saw and talked with Kim, Heid Erdrich, Denise Sweet, and Gordon Henry. We moved our conversation to the area where we were supposed to read. Each one of us read our poetry, poured our words out to the assembled crowd of about eighty people. I think we connected with the audience and each other. It was good.

The week after the Milwaukee gig, we assembled to read again. It was a slightly different cast this time.

Noted author Gerald Vizenor was there, as were Kim and Heid. Doyle Turner also shared his words at Birchbark Books, the setting for this reading. I wonder where we wandering Ojibwe poets will meet to read again?

My connection with *Older Than America*, the movie, started with a phone call from Riki McMasters of the Minnesota Film Board. She said she was with people who were making a movie and were scouting locations in this area. Riki asked if she could come to the World Headquarters of the Fond du Lac Follies. When she did, she came with director Georgina Lightning. We had coffee inside then went outside to hang around the fire pit. Ray Earley was there spinning stories. He had a brand new audience. There was a news conference held at the Black Bear Casino and Georgina Lightning and producer Christina Walker spoke about the film. While talking with Georgina about the movie, I learned she rewrote the script to include my fire pit and house in the movie.

The film company will be shooting on and near the Fond du Lac Reservation for about a month. People are always asking me what the movie is about, and I tell them I don't know because I haven't seen a script. I did hear some key words however, words like *boarding school, earthquake*, an art teacher who looks exactly like Georgina Lightning, and Adam Beach, who looks exactly like Adam Beach.

I have come to call anyone associated with the movie the Hollywoods. Yup, the Hollywoods. We have been in almost daily contact with the Hollywoods. We also run into them at the Black Bear Hotel and Casino since that is where they are staying while here on the Rez. There must be thirty or forty of them Hollywoods running around.

On the first official day of shooting, one of the Hollywoods called and asked if I would come and say a few words before they got started. I replied that I would be honored to do that. I got there and it looked just like a movie set. They had a camera set up on little railroad tracks, they had lights and filters for the lights, they had big trucks parked all over the street, they had a sound system and microphones, and they had cables snaking around. There must have been twenty-five Hollywoods standing around behind the camera. For a little while there I became one of them Hollywoods.

I asked Bobby Darin, whose name is Dan Harrison, what was happening with the scene. He explained that Wes Studi's character would arrive and get out of his car and walk up and talk with Glen Gould's character. What? Wes Studi was in this movie, too? I have long been a fan of his work, and now I would be able to see him act in person. Wes Studi came up and shook my hand and thanked me for my words and said he liked my books. I shook back and told him how I admired his work. I watched for a while then left before the acting and shooting was done. I came home and told my wife I had just met Wes Studi. She said who? I took her to the Internet and showed her his film biography and picture. She said she wasn't really a movie person.

That evening we met with the Hollywoods at the Black Bear Casino. Wes came into the Lady Slipper and joined our table. Ray Earley and I began trading stories with Wes, the Vietnam vet. Ray, Wes, Pat, and I and a bunch of Hollywoods went to a quieter place to continue our visiting. Wes said people like Pat, who didn't know his movies, would keep him humble. She asked why he went to Vietnam. He said he wanted to see if he could handle it, being in a war. Ray and I learned he was in the army and was a radio man in the Delta. Our visit was just good.

The Hollywoods will also shoot part of the movie by the fire pit in the yard. The fire pit we use for boiling maple sap and parching wild rice. It seems only natural for that fire pit to be in the movie. The story for that scene is Adam Beach's character comes up to the fire, where Ray, Patricia, and I are sitting while telling stories. Adam Beach? I haven't even met him yet. I think there will be more about *Older Than America* in the Follies.

Chapter 6

Pretending to Be Actors—2007

The cast and crew of the film *Older Than America* have completed their work on this Reservation. Now we have to wait for a year and a half before we can see the finished product.

I got a call from one of the Hollywoods telling me I had to report to the Ojibwe school for my first time in front of the camera. They were shooting a couple of scenes on one of the trails in the area known as The Forestry and were using the school as a staging area.

I walked into the gym and quickly observed that at least a hundred other people got the call. Even Catherine Whipple of *The Circle* newspaper was there. I was milling around with the gaggle of extras when one of the Hollywoods told me to go to the makeup room. I sat on the chair, and the makeup woman began to work on my mug shot, my face. She put a little bib inside my collar as she unlimbered her tools. She brushed powder on with a big brush, matched my skin tone with one of her creams, and began rubbing it in trying to make me pretty. I thought it was the same as putting lipstick on a pig. She told me it was to knock the shine off of my greasy face.

One of the Hollywoods shuttled me to the scene of the scenes. I walked into the field and scanned around.

There were warm-up tents, lights, the camera's little railroad tracks were laid, and there were more people milling around. They also had fires inside some oil barrels. It was a good thing because the temp was about nine above. As I saw it, the scene went like this . . . two people arrive and walk through a crowd to a drum. I saw Amik standing in the crowd, looking cold and stoic at the same time.

I watched the professionals work. The cast and crew worked hard in the cold of a Minnesota winter. These Hollywoods were good. Dan Harrison thought it would look good if Dennis Banks's character draped a blanket around the woman as she was welcomed back to the community. They needed a Pendleton blanket. Them Hollywoods had a lot of stuff, but they didn't have any Pendletons. I celled Pat and she brought two blankets to the doings. Pat and I pretended to be actors and welcomed that woman back home. I think we both got some serious face time on camera. Wow, in the same shot with Adam Beach and Tantoo Cardinal, Glen Gould and Gloria Eshkibok. We did the scene many times until director Georgina Lightning and assistant director Rowdy were happy with our acting. The actors warmed up in the little warm-up tents between takes. It was getting cold after standing many hours in the snow. When we were released, Pat and I escaped to the casino, where we warmed up around a couple of keno machines.

The Hollywoods arrived in Sawyer at 0600 hours with their semitrucks and trailers. They filled Northrup Road, north to south. The Hollywoods quickly turned our house and yard into a movie set. I didn't count, but I estimated at least fifty of them all doing their work.

They had lights and cables, cameras and microphones. They began shooting at the fire pit. In preparing the set, the Hollywoods used concrete logs and a propane flame for the fire. It looked like a fire, but it didn't give off heat. I heard someone say, "Colder Than America?"

The makeup women arrived and set up their lights and chairs. They powdered and creamed everyone who was going to be in the shot at the fire pit. This was Ray Earley's first time on camera. After one take, Georgina came up and told Ray he was supposed to look at the other people around the fire and not just smile at the camera. In this scene, I actually had lines to deliver. Here they are: "Why, you got a crime to report or are the cops looking for you, too?" And then later, while sitting around the cold fire, I say: "A geologist, huh? What brings you around these parts?" The cast members hung around inside the house keeping warm. Adam Beach fell asleep on our couch. His wife, Tara, said she has many pictures of Adam asleep on other movie sets.

Enrolled Fonjalackers got a gift from Venezuela again. This gift was international in scope, nation to nation. From Hugo Chavez of Venezuela, to Citgo Corporation, to the Minnesota Cbippewa Tribe, to the Fond du Lac Band of Lake Superior Chippewa, to me. The gift was for five hundred bucks worth of warm. For the second time, Chavez gave us credit that could be used for whatever one uses for heat in the winter. We use propane, so the Fond du Lac Propane Company will get our gift. Others use electricity, oil, or wood. As that old saying goes, warm is warm; okay, okay, it isn't an old saying but it is true anyway. I know Venezuela and the United States don't call each other niijii (friend), but the gift of warm was good. Apparently, Hugo Chavez doesn't blame us for Bush or his icy policies. I don't think the gift of warm should be used in the political world. Acceptance of this gift doesn't mean I agree with the policies of either Venezuela or the United States. But the warm is so warm. So, Hugo Chavez, I'd like to thank you from the bottom of my warm bottom. When you read the Follies, you will know your gift was appreciated here in this northern Minnesota Reservation.

I read something in the newspaper that I am still having a hard time understanding. Shortly after the Iraq war started, I read how the United States sent money to help in the war effort. They shipped 363 tons of new shrink-wrapped bundles of $100 bills to Iraq. That is 726,000 pounds of Franklins. I am still trying to put that in perspective. I was having trouble grasping how much 363 tons of money is, so my friend Ray Earley did some number crunching. Say I can haul a half ton of money in my silver Silverado: it would take 726 trips. Say I was hauling it to the docks in Duluth, thirty miles away. If I hauled one load a day, seven days a week, it would take four days short of two years to tote that much money. It would take 5,445 gallons of gasoline @ $2.35 a gallon. The gasoline alone would cost $12,795.75. Now we're talking some real money here. I wonder what one could buy with a ton of money? I also wonder what 363 tons bought in Iraq?

Jonathon Schulze was a young Marine who served in Iraq with an infantry company. After he returned from the war, he was having trouble dealing with the aftereffects and felt suicidal. He asked the VA for help twice and was told he was twenty-sixth on the list for an open bed. He couldn't wait, and he hung himself.

The whole situation reminds me of my return from the Vietnam War. I went to the VA and asked for help. I was turned away and referred to a doctor in the community. That didn't work out so pretty good because during our sessions together all I heard about were his problems. I stopped seeing him because I really couldn't afford to give him almost half of my paycheck at the time, and we weren't talking about my problems associated with my service in the war. Six weeks later, I read in the newspaper how my shrink shot himself. Later, on my own, I discovered that writing about the war helped me. It really did.

My newspaper tells me the governors in the Midwest surrounding the Great Lakes have signed a compact about how to use the waters from those lakes. I didn't read about any tribal groups being involved in the compact. I think the Anishinaabeg should have been included in that decision because if they start selling Lake Superior water to folks in the dry southwest, it will affect my treaty rights. They can't sell something that isn't totally theirs.

There is a new face on Northrup Road. Rizal moved in across the road from us shortly after he was born. The newest resident is named after a national hero of the Philippines—José Rizal. Rizal's parents, Sarah and Jeff, are smiling just hard. I didn't know anything about any national hero from the Philippines, so I googled him and learned quite a bit about this remarkable man. He was born in 1861, learned the alphabet when he was three, and became a medical doctor in 1877. He mastered twenty-two languages and was an artist, surveyor, teacher, poet, linguist, musician, architect, theologist, and nationalist. In a poem of his called "Mother Tongue," one line says, "One who doesn't love his mother tongue is worse than a putrid fish and beast." He also said, "While a people preserve its language, it preserves liberty." José Rizal was shot by the Spanish and Catholic leaders during the revolution in the Philippines. He died in 1896. I wonder where the moccasins of the Northrup Road Rizal will go?

I was able to teach my grandson, the one I call Bimose, how to count, ojibwemo agindaasod. He stops here every school morning, and we count in Ojibwe. Bimose can count to twenty, frontward and backward, can count to ninety by tens. I told him when he can count to ninety-nine without a mistake, I will teach him what comes next. Some Shinnob said some chilling words when he said: with the language you are Anishinaabe, without it you are descendants of the Anishinaabe. So, Fonjalackers—which one are you? A descendant?

Sugar bush is rapidly approaching. The usual signs are there: the melted snow at the base of the trees, the return of the crows. The warm sun, the relatively warm days and cool nights are also another clue. We are preparing here. I have to make about thirty taps to replace the ones that wore out. The taps usually last four to five years. We are also cutting dry wood. Once again my favorite kind of wood is dry standing maple trees, the Cadillacs of firewood. My son Jimmy is preparing, and this year, for the first time, my son Joe will have his own sugar bush. I am glad I was able to teach my sons the little I know about making syrup. I think Matthew and Jackie will be the main helpers again this year; son Calvin will also help. Who knows who else? I am looking forward to sitting around the fire, soaking up the physical and spiritual warmth. Since the maple syrup is a gift from the Creator, I never worry about how much I get. It varies from year to year—one year I got three gallons of syrup; the following year I got twenty-four gallons.

My family and I tapped maple trees where my grampa Mike Shabiash used to tap. I felt good about it because I know we are probably tapping the same trees he used. Before tapping, we offered tobacco to thank Gichi Manidoo for the gift of maple sap. Using an electric drill, we made the holes, cleaned them out, tapped a tap in, and hung a milk jug. On the second day, we tapped another fifty trees. Barb Rordak helped this time. It was her first time at a sugar bush, and she was eager to learn how we do things. On the third day, we rested and let the trees do all the work. We prepared the fire pit, dug it about eighteen inches deep, built a fire so we would have a bed of coals. We hung the kettle from the iskigamiziganakik, filled it with sap, and sat around the fire. I suspended a piece of bacon over the boiling liquid to prevent boilovers, and we just waited. When the level of the sap dropped down, we added more. We kept doing this until we were out of sap. We watched the sap gradually turning browner. I began tasting the sap as it approached the syrup stage. Once it was close, we carried it inside for the final boil and filtering. It took us all day to make three gallons of syrup. The heat of the fire stays with you long after you walk away from the fire pit. The house smells sweet as the final boil is happening. We filter our syrup at least six times. Then the fun part begins. We fill small jars with syrup and pass them out to relatives who are too old to make syrup anymore. Two of my sons had their own sugar bush. Jimmy has been making syrup with his son Niiwin for a few years now. This was Joseph's first time doing it at his house. He and his friend Kak tapped, gathered, and boiled their own syrup. I liked the smile on Joseph's face when he offered his son, Bimose, the first taste of their syrup. It is magic: we make food from trees. We ended up with ten gallons of syrup for the year but are bragging twelve.

LCpl. Harry H. Timberlake, USMC, age twenty, a Marine from Minong, Wisconsin, died in Iraq's Anbar province. We grieve with his family and friends. Counting dead Marines is getting sickening for this old jarhead. Can anyone tell me why LCpl. Timberlake gave up his future?

Naria is her name and she is our latest granddaughter, the newest face on Northrup Road, even newer than Rizal across the road. Joseph and Sara are the parents, and Naria joins a family already in progress. Just think, she will be able to brag to her grandchildren that she grew up next door to the World Headquarters of the Fond du Lac Follies. We call her Ziinzibakwadaabookwe.

Ezigaa and I woke up the hibernating Corvette. He checked the air pressure in the tires while I put fresh gasoline in the tank. I was carefully pouring the gas in, didn't want to spill any on the pretty paint, when it started glugging and came out in spurts. Splash, all over the paint. I jammed the spout into the tank NASCAR style and poured the rest in. Ezigaa hooked up the charger to the battery, and we waited. Once the battery was charged, I got in and turned the key. The starter motor sounded for a couple of seconds before the familiar roar of the big V-8 engine.

I am looking forward to making wild rice fanning baskets this year. For the Northrup family, this is an annual activity. We have been doing this for many years, and we have taught many people how to work with the materials. Two of my sons went to the woods to find good birch bark for me. Aaron and Joseph walked a lot, and they reported they were not lost because they knew they were still in northern Minnesota. They just didn't know exactly where their car was parked. It took them hours to find it so they could bring the bark home. They also neglected to check the weather channel, and they were both damp when they got home. I have one student who wants to learn how to work with the materials we use. He is Brad Northrup, my nephew. He is learning step-by-step how we construct a fanning basket. We went to the woods and gathered green willow. We peeled and tied two pieces together, bent them, then hung them in the sun to dry. We also peeled basswood bark for the stitching. My godson Zac also brought us some good birch bark. He said it's because we taught him how to work with birch bark. He is also gathering birch for himself so he can make his makakoon.

Question: What did Ray Earley tell you?
Answer: Gaawiin wiikaa debwetaw wa'aw boogidi.

Fand du Lac Follies motored to the east. The occasion was the Independence Day parade held in Cloquet. The '64 Corvette was finally out of the shop so we wanted to be a part of the parade. My granddaughter Raina wanted to be in the parade, so she perched on the trunk lid. I told her the parade was for her and her part was to wave at the crowds. The nine-year-old was smiling and waving. As we were preparing the car, I noticed a bald eagle flying overhead as if he were checking us out. I thought that was a good beginning to the parade. Two air force jets also flew over. Call me old-fashioned, but I was more impressed with the eagle. The cheering got loud when we came by groups of Fonjalackers. I saw my grandson Bimose waving at us. My sister Nita and her family were in the crowd waving. The parade was fun and we enjoyed ourselves. The entire parade route was eight blocks. It seemed like it was over too quickly, so I circled around and rejoined the parade. We tucked in between the fire trucks at the end. The Shinnobs were laughing when they saw us coming by the second time. I told my cousin Les Northrup I was getting paid mileage. I wasn't really, but it was good for a laugh.

Next, Fond du Lac Follies motored to the Something Annual Veterans Powwow held here in Sawyer. My wife was going to operate her food stand called Stand Here. This year she had a sign that said Free Coffee for Veterans. Those business classes she is taking at Fond du Lac Tribal and Community College are kicking in, especially the marketing ones. I set up my stand to sell books and big birch bark baskets—didn't have a cutesy name for it. My stand had a bingo table across the front that held the books and baskets. The rest of the shelter was a veterans' lounge; we had chairs and shade, stories and lies, a Marine Corps flag, a John Wayne picture, and free coffee from Stand Here. USMC vet Ray Earley had a captive audience for his stories. He had the largest chair and the only footrest. George Dick had a giveaway on Saturday morning. His son Kak gave me a new red Marine Corps hat. I think he wanted me to change the oil in my old one. One vet visit was pretty special. It was Adam, a young Marine just back from Iraq. He was a gunner on a Humvee and was only blown up once by a roadside bomb. I asked Adam if he wanted a Corvette ride. He said yes, and we left the powwow grounds at Mash-Ka-Wisen to cruise the curvy roads south of Sawyer. According to Mary Northrup, there were 157 Fond du Lac veterans, 105 vets from other places.

At the end of the powwow they had fireworks. To a combat vet with PTSD, fireworks are like bringing a keg of beer to an AA picnic, or a Corvette to a Thunderbird car show, a cat to a pit bull dogfight. Ray and I went to my house. The explosions weren't as loud, but we could still hear them, the thunk sound when they left the tube, the explosions when they went off in the air. The rapid small explosions said *Ambush!* When they stopped, I thought everyone was changing magazines. If they have fireworks again, I shall go to the woods.

After the powwow, Fond du Lac Follies jetted to the Left Coast. I broke my no-flying vow because the trip to California was necessary. I was going out to meet a longtime friend and fellow Marine, Walter Rosales. I was there to spend some time with him and his family. I first met Walter when he joined India Company, 3rd Battalion, 9th Marines in An Hoa, South Vietnam, in April 1966. We both survived our time in the bush. I came home and got out; Walter still had time on his enlistment and later went back to Vietnam for a second tour with India Company, 3rd Battalion, 27th Marines. He survived that tour also. We didn't see each other for more than twenty years, until one day when we met at the Vietnam Wall in Washington, DC. We shook hands and talked about our time in the war. We also talked about life after the war, including our families. Walter and I stayed in touch by telephone. Patricia and I were in San Diego, and I called Walter. We got together and had a good visit. Some years later, Walter and his son Dean came to Sawyer for a visit. Since they were desert Indians, I took them to the lake for a canoe ride. I paddled Walter around for a while, and then Dean wanted to try paddling a canoe. He learned how quickly a canoe can tip over. Patricia went to San Diego for a conference and she and Walter traded wild rice for grapefruit. Last year, Walter called and said Dean died unexpectedly.

A few weeks ago, Walter's daughter April called and invited me for the memorial ceremony they were going to have for Dean. I quickly agreed and immediately forgot about my no-flying vow. In addition to my normal fear of flying, I was unsure if my name was on the government's no-fly list. I showed my picture ID and e-ticket to the TSA person. She said, "Hi, Jim. I was in Rick Smith's class when you came to the University of Minnesota at Duluth for a reading of your poetry." I felt better already and went through the screening process. When I got to Palm Springs, there was a driver holding a sign that said Jim Northrup. I felt the desert heat right away. The radio said it was going to be 112 degrees. Walter came to the Fantasy Springs Casino and Hotel and we visited. Shortly after that, we went to his daughter's house for some southwest cuisine. After visiting, Walter took me to the hotel, and we agreed to meet for breakfast. Before I went in, Walter told me there are two kinds of Indians in California: there are the 7-Eleven and the dot Indians, or the ponytail and casino Indians.

We ate breakfast, and Walter took me on a tour. We went up a curvy mountain road; it might be called Palms to Pine Highway. There must have been twenty S curves on that road. Walter said that road was used in the movie *It's a Mad, Mad, Mad, Mad World*. I was wishing I had my Corvette for that road. It was a lot cooler up there. We enjoyed the wind as we shot the breeze. That evening we went to the ceremony held at the Cabazon graveyard. They do things a little different than the Anishinaabe, but the thoughts and feelings were the same. We ate at a feast, and I listened to the singers and joined in the dancing. It was all gourds, no drums at all. I met the chairman of the Cabazon people and thanked them for what they did for Indian gambling. I am glad I was able to be there for my friend. I know he would have done the same for me. Marines are like that, especially those who have shared combat time. I sure was glad to get back to the cool air of northern Minnesota. I had parked the Corvette at my son's house. Matthew and Jackie said they heard the car whimpering because no one was driving it.

Beneshiikwe, Raina, came to stay with us for a while. She is nine years old and livens up this house. She is a girly girl. When she wants something from me, all she does is ask me in her little girl voice, tilts her head toward one shoulder, smiles into my eyes, and says, "Please, grampa," and I give in every time. Raina is in the third grade, and I can tell she will not have much trouble in school. She reads well above her grade level, and I can hardly wait to introduce her to some of the things I have written. Yup, living with Beneshiikwe brightens up this place.

I also have a seven-year-old grandson who lives next door. One morning, Bimose said, "Grampa, did you know I have never had a twenty-dollar bill of my own."

I replied, "Oh."

A little bit later he said, "I'd sure like to have a twenty-dollar bill."

"Me, too," I said.

Finally, he came right out and said, "Grampa, would you give me a twenty-dollar bill?"

"Yes," I said, "when you can count from one to fifty in Ojibwemowin without making a mistake."

In the past few years, we have been counting in Ojibwemowin, and he is also learning Ojibwe words and phrases, so I thought he could do it. The look in his eyes said he knew he could do it, too. The next morning he began counting. He got to twenty-three before he skipped a number. I made a buzzer noise to signal him I had heard a mistake. The next morning he got to thirty-two before he repeated a number and heard my buzzer. He kept trying every morning for a week and a half; he was getting closer and closer to fifty. On that final morning, his eyes showed that he knew he could do it successfully. He began smiling as he said forty-four, forty-five, forty-six. His smile was getting bigger as he said forty-seven, forty-eight, forty-nine. He took a deep breath and said fifty. I said, "Mii gwayak." He yelled, "I did it!" I peeled off a twenty and handed it to him. He asked if he could call his mom to tell her. I said, "Go ahead, goat head."

The next morning I told him I would give him another twenty dollar bill if he could count to a hundred in Ojibwe without a mistake. Before we started on that one I asked him to count to a hundred by tens. He did that easily enough. It took him three days before he earned the second twenty. Once again he yelled, "I did it!" He called his mom to tell her he had earned another twenty dollars. For the final exam in counting in Ojibwe, I told him I would give him a twenty-dollar bill if he could count backward from fifty. It took him two days before I gave him the last twenty I had. That boy and I are doing something together that counts.

Fond du Lac Follies motored to Saint Paul to see Jim Northrup in a museum. The event was the premier showing of the exhibits at the Minnesota History Museum. The exhibit was called Minnesota 150. The purpose of the exhibit was to help celebrate Minnesota's sesquicentennial. My part of the doings was a poem called "Ditched" for the topic of Indian boarding schools. To go along with the poem, I made a little crawler toy we used to make in Pipestone boarding school. I wrote that we didn't have any toys at boarding school so we had to make our own. Pipestone wasn't a toy kind of a place. My poem was chosen from a field of 2,760 nominations. The Fond du Lac Reservation is four years older than the State of Minnesota. Welcome to the neighborhood, kid.

My son Aaron Ezigaa needed to go to Duluth for an eye exam so he could get his driver's permit. He had earlier passed the written part of the test. I picked him up from school, and he got into that beautiful '64 Corvette. On the freeway trip to Duluth, I began pounding his ears with driving tips and tried to sound wisdomful. He listened. I went inside to help ease his way through the bureaucratic process. The bureaucrat behind the counter turned out to be related to Bouda, one of the Reservation Business Committee members. He gave Aaron the eye test, took his picture, and took ten dollars from me. I asked when it would be legal for Aaron to drive. The bureaucrat told me he would be legal as soon as he walked out the door. When we got outside, I gave Aaron the Corvette keys and told him to take me home. He looked at me to see if I was kidding. When I got into the passenger seat, I could see the grin beginning on his face. He got behind the steering wheel, buckled his seat belt, carefully adjusted the mirrors, and fired that big loud motor up. He casually drove through the traffic on the Duluth streets until he got to the freeway. He was smiling big as he eased into the traffic on the interstate. He smiled for the next thirty-five miles on the way home, then I told him it was time to put the Corvette away for the winter.

The next day, my son drove me to the Reservation's C-store where we gassed up (20 cents off a gallon for Fond du Lac Band members) and washed the outside of the Corvette. We toweled it dry then motored to Brookston for the community powwow. Aaron Ezigaa sat in the Corvette driver seat while I went in to boozhoo everyone I knew. I saw my cousin Duunk, Lee Staples, Bouda Smith, and cousin Chetty enjoying the doings. When we got home, Aaron put the fuel stabilizer in and covered the car with a canvas tarp. Next, we shall jack it up to take the weight off the tires and bearings. The final act for preparing for winter is to put mothballs in the car to keep the mice from eating the wires. Earlier this year I wrote that I had made a ricer; this month I made a Corvette driver.

Fond du Lac Follies motored to the community center here in Sawyer for the quarterly meeting of the Reservation Business Committee. It is one of four times a year when Fond du Lac voters can meet with their leaders in an almost forumlike setting. The chair, Karen Diver, was sitting at the table facing the audience. She was flanked by Ferd Martineau, the secretary-treasurer, and Sandra Shabiash, the Sawyer representative. I was related to two-thirds of the leaders. The Fond du Lac voters faced them from their rows of chairs. The chair explained that the representatives from Cloquet, Gene Reynolds and Brookston's Bouda Smith, were at meetings out of state. Nitaawis Rick Defoe opened the meeting by smoking his pipe and speaking Ojibwe to the people. The meeting began and quickly fell off the agenda wagon because the Fond du Lac voters had questions and wanted answers from their leaders. The questions were mostly about job policies and financial matters. At times, the questions were quite shrill. The RBC members answered the questions as best they could. I noticed they were making notes when tough questions were asked. One angry voter walked toward the leaders and as part of her question said she was going to slap Karen Diver. The other voters grumbled and growled at her and she quickly added . . . with a lawsuit. The almost endless questions continued for several hours. The RBC members tried to answer each one. I know from watching the RBC meetings in the past that most leaders would have declared the meeting out of order and banged a gavel to end it. This group of leaders talked with the voters and continued talking as we were all walking to our cars. Two things I gleaned from the meeting are: voters wanted these meetings monthly and want all of their leaders there.

Chapter 7

The Results Were Not So Pretty Good—2008

My son Jim is a road man for the Native American Church. That is not my system of religious beliefs, but I have seen the positive changes in his life since he began practicing that way of believing. As the old saying goes, the proof is in the pudding. If you stopped by Jim's house and were hungry, he would give you the last of his pudding. Jim wanted to have a birthday meeting for his oldest son, Jim. He asked for permission to use the Sawyer Community Center. Under the previous administration, his requests were always granted. This time his request was denied because, in the words of the RBC, the Native American Church is "not from around here."

Let us look a little closer at this statement. The Big Drum ceremonies that used to be held in Sawyer were not from around here. Those songs and ceremonies came from the Dakota people. The Catholic Church is not from around here, either. I think that came from Rome, Italy, with the Jesuits. The other Christian religions practiced on this Reservation come from Germany and England, I believe. In pursuing his request, Jim tried to inform members of the RBC about the Native American Church. In my research, I learned there are between 250,000 to

400,000 members of that church in the United States. Also I learned that the US Congress said members of the Native American Church were the only people legally allowed to use peyote. The Catholic Church recently used the Cloquet Community Center to hold their annual bazaar, as they have in years past. The message I am getting from this RBC is that American white guys' religions are good and the Native American Church is bad. I do know the Reservation offices are closed down for Christmas and Easter, two Christian holidays. The Rez store and casinos stay open, however. The executive director of the Reservation, Mike Himango, informed my son he could not use any of the Reservation facilities to hold his prayer meeting. I told Jim he could use my house for his birthday meeting. We moved the furniture out of the living room and kitchen, and about thirty people showed up for this meeting of the Native American Church. The people prayed and sang all night. In the morning, they ate together. What is wrong with singing and praying? I believe my son's rights were violated by the Reservation Business Committee under the American Indian Religious Freedom Act and the Indian Civil Rights Act. What the hell is going on here?

Reports of my recent heart attack were greatly exaggerated. As part of my annual physical at the Minoayaawin Clinic, I took an EKG test. There was one squiggly line on the chart the medical people didn't like. They thought I had a silent heart attack. They arranged a series of heart tests for me. It took a couple of weeks to get them scheduled and completed. I wore a heart monitor for twenty-four hours, had an ultrasound reading on my heart. That one showed no damage to the valves and walls. I was also supposed to take a stress test at a hospital in Duluth. The man taking the test in front of me died during his stress test. They asked if I still wanted to go through with it. I said sure, what are the odds of two people dying back-to-back during the tests. I didn't study for that stress test but passed anyway. They took pictures of my heart from many different angles. I met with a cardiologist after the tests were done. She reviewed the tests and told me I didn't have a heart attack. She instructed me in what symptoms to watch for. I got another EKG as a going away present. And as Cher used to sing . . . and the beat goes on.

Fond du Lac Follies motored to Gakaabikaang, or, as some people like to call it, Minneapolis. Of course I drove that shiny Corvette. I was invited south by Rick Gresczyk to talk to his Native American literature class at Metro Community and Technical College. We went to the classroom. I introduced myself to the students in Ojibwe, and Rick translated it into English. I like to do that because speaking Ojibwe calms my stage fright. I knew the students had read my first book. It was easy to slip into my storytelling mode, so I did. I began by telling the students about the federal boarding school system. I told them I was six when I first rode the school bus to Pipestone. My older sister Judy was in the second grade. I knew my alphabet and could count to ninety-nine;

Judy wouldn't tell me the next number after ninety-nine. In those days, before telephones came to the Rez, our only way of staying connected with family was by letter. I didn't know how to write. Pauline Moose, an older girl, helped me write my "Dear Maw, How are you, I am fine" letters. She also showed me how to mail them. I have never forgotten her kindness in helping me when I was a little guy. Over the years, when our trails crossed again, I would give her a pound of rice, a jar of maple syrup, or a book as my way of thanking her for helping me. She was one of the very few good memories of my time at that depressing, culture-robbing boarding school three hundred miles from home.

After a break, we went back to the classroom, where I continued talking about Native American literature. Just for grins I asked the class if they could name any other Anishinaabeg writers. The results were not so pretty good. I helped them along by giving them the names of Louise Erdrich, Heid Erdrich, Lise Erdrich, Gerald Vizenor, Marcie Rendon, the Treuer brothers, Gordon Henry, Kim Blaeser, Don Two Rivers, Doyle Turner Jr., Mark Turcotte, Jamison Mahto, Al Everywhere Hunter, Margaret Noori. Then I told them my dog stories and gave them some questions from the Follies. Before I left the classroom, some of the students lined up to get my autograph.

After that visit with students, I headed north, home to the Rez. I stopped at Tobies in Hinkles. A young Indian guy was admiring that Corvette. He asked if I was Jim Northrup; I confessed that I was. He said his maw was Pauline Moose. He said she was just talking about knowing Jim Northrup because she used to write his letters for him. He said he just called her, she was awake and at home. I drove to her house. We visited, and I again thanked her for writing my letters home for me. She said she had a secret. She said I didn't know it, but at the bottom of all those letters, she wrote "Please send cookies." She said she was carrying that secret for a long time. We were telling the same story at about the same time but were seventy-five miles apart. Her story was better because she had more details.

Al Franken came to Nagaajiwanaang. Yup, Fond du Lac. He is the only politician to come to this Reservation this election season. The last one I remember was Mark Dayton, who came in seventh in a six-candidate race. I asked some Fonjalackers who they were going to vote for in the upcoming election, Franken or Coleman? One guy wondered why I thought he would vote for a lantern. When Al arrived, my son Matthew and his partner Jackie and I were sitting in the front row, left of the center aisle, of course. When Al was done with his stump speech, he asked for questions. I quickly raised my hand, and he called on me. I told him this was a softball question. I told him I had met his wife a few years back at a *Circle* newspaper fund-raiser. She was admiring my birch bark baskets. After looking at them closely, she decided not to buy one. I finished by asking Al if he thought she had changed her mind about buying one of my baskets. Al said he would buy it for her since she was working so hard on his campaign. I sat back knowing I would vote for Al Franken.

A hearing on a petition to remove Karen Diver our esh-paabid (highest leader) was well attended by the Fond du Lac people. The petition said she had overstepped her authority when she forgave part of a loan to a family member of a former RBC man. The setting was the gym at the Cloquet Community Center. There were four tables with chairs at one end of the gym. One was for four RBC members, one was for Karen Diver, one was for two court clerks and attorney Henry Buffalo, and the fourth table was for the tribal judge. There were rows of chairs for the people of Fond du Lac, the Fonjalackers. Some sat in the chairs, some chose to sit in the bleachers. One Fonjalacker wanted to know why Henry Buffalo was there. He explained that he was representing the RBC. Right away I wondered where our crack Rez lawyer Dennis Peterson was. He usually represents the RBC in legal matters. As a Fonjalacker, I wondered how much money was paid to Henry Buffalo for his representation. Buffalo is long remembered as the attorney working for the RBC when the sale of the 1854 treaty was negotiated. Like most of those attending, I wanted to hear the evidence of her alleged wrongdoing. My three sons and I had signed the petition for a hearing. The new judge opened the proceedings and told us no other evidence would be allowed at the hearing. The RBC members could only use the petition in their deliberations. For me, it was difficult to understand the judge because she was an um speaker: every third or fourth word was "um." Pretty soon all I was hearing was her "um." After a while, the entire RBC left the hearing room and were gone for about an hour while they were making a decision. The RBC came back in and announced their findings. The vote was for dismissal of all charges on all counts. The vote was unanimous. Karen Diver abstained from voting. As the people left, my son Jim asked me if we had signed the moo list. I told him I thought we had.

―――――――――――――――――――――――

The most recent Thursday-night Ojibwe language table was well attended. It was their first meeting of the new year. By my count, there were more than twenty humans that showed up to speak and learn more of our ancient language. It was a good feeling. Dan Jones, our teacher from the Fond du Lac Tribal and Community College, was there with his knowledge and humor. Fonjalacker Chuck Smith Jr. prayed with tobacco and wa'aw manido-miijim. After the meal, which included wild rice, chicken, veggie snacks, a mac salad, and sweets, we begin to use Ojibwe. Dan started off by getting everyone to raise their hand and swear they would not use English for the rest of the evening. He then asked different people to introduce themselves in Ojibwe. The students said their name, their clan, and where they were from. Dan then asked us questions after each speaker was done. We took turns trying to answer using only Ojibwe. It was a learning experience because we had to listen and pronounce unfamiliar words.

―――――――――――――――――――――――

Once again, Hugo Chavez of Venezuela gave us a Christmas gift of warmth. It was either a late Christmas or an early Christmas, depending on whether you look behind or ahead on the calendar. Thanks, Hugo. The gift of warmth was spread out among more Shinnobs than last year. I learned that the Red Lake Reservation had recently joined the pool of skins getting the gift of warmth from Hugo. So Hugo, when you read the Follies, you can see one Fonjalacker wants to say apiijigo miigwech.

Fond du Lac Follies motored to Duluth to be part of an antiwar panel. My son Aaron Ezigaa did the driving. The cold was measured at below zero. We got there a bit early and hung around and watched the activists arrive. I spoke in Ojibwe, and after my introduction, I introduced Aaron Ezigaa to the crowd and told them he was seventeen and my main reason for being antiwar. Then I recited several Vietnam-related poems to illustrate how that war had affected me and was still affecting me some forty years later.

In February, Fond du Lac Follies motored to Duluth again. The occasion was a chance to hear authors Heid and Lise Erdrich. These two Anishinaabe women have a sister named Louise who also writes books. Is this the Shinnob version of the Brontë sisters? I knew Heid and her works because we had shared the stage a couple of times, most recently at Birchbark Books, in

Minneapolis. She was up on the podium when I walked in. She recognized me and waved. I threw her a Sawyer wave in return. Linda LeGarde Grover of UMD introduced the speakers. Heid went first and recited some of her favorite poems. I enjoy her words and the way she puts them together. I had never heard or even met Lise but was eager to see what she does with words. She read from some of her short fiction, and I could see the audience liked what she said. I found myself chuckling at times. I joined the line of people who were eager to buy their books. The Anishinaabe have always been good storytellers, and these two should be included in any list of someone worth reading and hearing.

An apology resolution was proposed as Section 8113 in the 2010 Defense Appropriations Act, HR 3326, Public Law No. 111-118. It is supposed "to officially apologize for the past ill-conceived policies by the US government toward the Native peoples of this land." The apology resolution states that the United States "apologizes on behalf of the people of the United States to all Native Peoples for the many instances of violence, maltreatment, and neglect inflicted on Native Peoples by citizens of the United States." First, what good would it do? Second, what good would it do? Third, what good would it do? An apology does not erase hundreds of years of genocide. The Jews were not the only ones who had a holocaust. We had one here, too.

Fond du Lac Follies motored to the Rez golf course club house for a wedding ceremony. My sister Susan Northrup and Ringo Starr, no, I mean Ringo Smith of Red Lake, made a major decision the other day. They have been going steady for the past thirty-seven years and decided to get married. After two kids and 444 months of learning about each other, they decided to take a chance and get hitched. As the older brother, I told Suzy no sense rushing into things, but there she was, looking good in a blue ribbon blouse, moccasins, and a skirt. What? My sister Suzy in a skirt? I haven't seen her in a skirt since she was a little girl. When she was changing from street shoes to moccasins, she crossed her legs, forgetting that she was wearing a skirt. She almost showed her unmentionables, almost became a blushing bride. Ringo looked resplendent in a matching ribbon shirt. This was an Ojibwe ceremony, and without going into too many details, it is enough to know there was a drum and singers, sweetgrass, an eagle wing fan, a pipe and tobacco, and a medicine man. Ringo had three men standing with him, Suzy had two women. At one point in the doings, we were given a chance to offer advice to the bride and groom. I heard my brother Vern warning Ringo about wooden nickels. I offered advice about tapping maple trees instead of basswood. I didn't hear what John Fineday told him. Suzy was getting advice from the two women standing with her.

After the doings we sat down to eat. A wedding ceremony is a good reason to have a feast, so we did. Members of the family brought food, and I ate and ate. There were two kinds of wild rice dishes, fry bread, potato salad, mashed potatoes, gravy, vegetables, fruit, Jell-O, and apple pie. The medicine man blessed the food and made a spirit dish. It felt good to gather with relatives and friends on this happy occasion. We passed babies around, told stories and lies, teased each other, and took many pictures. All four of my sons were there, Jim, Matthew, Joseph, and Aaron, and my two brothers Vern and Russ. I hugged my grandson Shabub and granddaughter Jalisa. After eating, we listened to the drum and singers. I think together we made this an event to remember. We wish for another thirty-seven years of bliss for those two. Geget gosha.

Fond du Lac Follies jetted to Lansing, Michigan, for Returning the Gift, Native Writers Conference. I wondered about that title. Is returning the gift the same as being an Indian giver? The event was presented by the Michigan State University American Indian studies program and Wordcraft Circle of Native Writers and Storytellers. When I arrived in Michigan, I set up camp in the Lansing Marriot, then I strolled over to the student union where the event was held. Right away I met Dr. Susan Krause, the director of the American Indian studies program. She introduced me to her helper Betsy Caldwell, who fixed me up with a schedule, meal tickets, and a short tour of our conference area. I got a little sign to hang around my neck that identified me as a presenter. Ten Native writers were selected to read from their works Thursday evening. I joined Eric Gansworth, Qwo-Li Driskill, Richard Van Camp, Pun Plamondon, Charlene Bearskin, Dr. Daniel Heath Justice, LeAnne

Howe, Debbie Reese, and her daughter Elizabeth Reese. Dr. David Treuer from Leech Lake was the final reader. During the in-between times, I got to meet other skin writers. Dr. Brenda Child of Red Lake was there. So was Helen Roy of Michigan. It was good to see Dr. LaVonne Ruoff also. I had met her fifteen to twenty years ago in Chicago. At that time she suggested I write my biography for publication in her American Indian Lives series. I told her I was too young and had a lot of living and writing to do. This time she told me it was time. My workshop was called "Ingii ozhibii'ige ezhi-waybak ishkoniganing, or How I saved Minnesota." My workshop had nothing to do with saving Minnesota; it was just a catchy title. I had writing exercises that illustrated character, setting, and plot. Thirty-five writers came to the class, and all of their heads were bent down writing for most of the class time. Dr. Margaret Noori was there. She teaches at the University in Ann Arbor. She has helped me with my writing and publishing before, and we met to do it again on a new book project of mine. The next morning we attended workshops by the Treuer brothers. David talked in the morning workshop. In his afternoon work-shop, Dr. Tony Treuer spoke mostly in Ojibwe. Actually, we four Minnesota Anishinaabeg authors outnumbered any other tribe. Do you think the next Indian Givers conference should be held in Minnesota?

It is warm and I saw the first drop of maple sap come through my tap. A sweet sugar bush story will be in the next Follies. Sugar bush has arrived again and we were prepared for it. Replacemet taps were carved, milk jugs were readied, and the buckets and barrels were put in the back of the truck. I assembled a good crew to help me with my 196 taps. My soon-to-be-eighteen-year-old son, Aaron Ezigaa, was anointed as this year's sugar bush master. This year we chose a sugar bush out in the Ditchbanks area of the Rez. I remember my grandfather used to move his sugar bush from year to year. I do the same thing. We went to the woods to tap the trees. The snow was knee-deep and it was like walking upstairs all day. We made trails from tree to tree. Some of the sap coming out of the trees spurted like a heartbeat. We gathered the sap and boiled it in the yard. The warm from the fire felt good.

The blizzard had been predicted for a couple of days. We were in a hurry to boil the 150 gallons of maple sap we had collected. My sugar bush crew was happy when we boiled the sap and completed that part of making syrup before the storm hit. The TV was telling me we were going to get two feet of snow with fifty-mile winds. The storm began with a single flake. The first to go was the broadband access. Oh no, not Internet access! How will I check my e-mail? A telephone call to the Technical Support Center revealed the problem was on their end somewhere, and they hoped to reestablish the connection within twenty-four to forty-eight hours. Great, do they know how long that is in Internet time? The ominous red light on the Advanced Networking Modem lets me know how fragile my link is to the rest of the world. The electricity flickers, and my computer shuts down. I am left here clicking the keys to a black screen. So far the computer always boots up so I can scrawl a few more words. I am typing as fast as I can between the computer and electrical failures. The satellite TV started making that static-y sound, nothing but snow on the screen. I got the signal it was trying to acquire the signal. The normal programs came back on, but the local channels were displaying a message that said they were aware their station was unavailable. One local TV station came back on, and I saw my son's school on the list of closed ones. The telephone rang, so I knew that machine was still working. It was my wife calling from a Reservation 125 miles west of mine. She was attending a workshop and told me about the blizzard there. The snowplow came by and sealed my driveways with a wall of snow. The snow is still falling, and the wind is still blowing hard. The local TV station reports a gust of sixty-three miles per hour. The police and TV people are telling everyone to stay home. No problem here. I got nowhere to go and a long time to get there, so I am nesting, going to hunker in my bunker. I cooked up a peanut butter/jelly/banana sandwich and settled down to watch the snow blow by in a horizontal manner. I guess sugar bush is on hold for a couple of days. Eventually, the storm abated (I like that word), and we went back to making maple syrup. We gathered and boiled, gathered friends and family around the fire while we were boiling. People came to learn how we make syrup, and we were happy to share what we know. When people ask how much we got we always say, enough for a Shinnob, not enough for a Chimook (Rez slang for "Americans").

In my travels I found a great singing group. Their name is Asani, and they sing songs that make me want to sing along. They sometimes use a rattle and a hand drum. The trio is composed of three women from Canada, Debbie Houle, Sherryl Sewepagaham, and Sarah Pocklington. They are Cree and Métis. I have made my family tired of listening to their music because I play the CD over and over. There are threats of the CD being held hostage until I agree not to play it so much. I can't help it, the music and the sound of their voices really appeal to me.

Later that spring, Fond du Lac Follies motored to Marquette, Michigan, for an Indigenous Environmental Network gathering. For this 250-mile one-way trip I brought out my favorite toy, the '64 Corvette. This was the first major trip of the year for that beautiful sports car. I gassed, greased, and washed the car. The directions were simple: hang a left in Superior, Wisconsin, then stay on the road until you get to Marquette. The Corvette rumbled along, eating the miles and drinking the gas. I know I was looking cool; it is too bad there are not many people in that part of Michigan who could see me being so cool. Once I arrived, I began meeting people I know. I met old friends and made new friends at the conference. In one workshop I learned what the people in Australia are doing to protect their lands. In another I learned how Anishinaabeg people are reseeding wild rice in Michigan. On the ride back to Minnesota, I ran into a rainstorm and learned I needed new weather-stripping because the car leaks.

Jennifer Neimi of the University of Minnesota at Duluth came out to Sawyer to visit during sugar bush. While she was here, she asked if we could perform the play *Shinnob Jep* for the Minnesota Indigenous Language Symposium IV. The doings were to be held at the Holiday Inn in downtown Duluth. I said sure, we can put on that play and make people laugh. The Northrup Road Players came into being at that point. I asked my son (and neighbor) Matthew if he wanted to play in the play again. His eyes lit up when he said yes. His partner, Jackie, said she would also like to act in *Shinnob Jep*. Nephew (and neighbor) Kris begged for a chance to be an actor, so the Northrup Road Players began rehearsal. We started ten days before the scheduled performance time. At first we practiced every other day, then we began daily rehearsals. Along the way we learned from each other how to better say and deliver the lines. We had a dress rehearsal at the Sawyer Center in front of a Mother's Day crowd. Despite theater tradition, none of us were wearing a dress, not even Jackie. We made the Sawyer women laugh when we did the play. One person was slightly confused and thought the play was an audience-participation kind of a show. As we were going through the questions and answers in the play, she would shout out her answers. It felt good to make those people laugh. On the day of the performance, the Northrup Road Players rehearsed twice and finished with the props. Meg Aerol, usually known as Dr. Margaret Noori, came to the symposium from Ann Arbor, Michigan. We had a good visit, and she drew some tipi poles for us. We needed the drawing for one of the signs used in the play.

Opening night, there must have been 250–280 people in the ballroom. The Northrup Road Players were ready. I wanted the lights to be dimmed and then turned back on to signal the opening of the play. The hotel staff got it half right; they turned the lights off, then didn't turn them back on for several minutes. I was trying to panic but didn't remember how. The audience patiently waited. The play began and our rehearsal time paid off because people started laughing. We were grooving on the feedback. The audience laughed all the way through the play. It seems like we just got started and the play was over. The Northrup Road Players did well, no major mistakes were made. I was thinking about this. In this time of a war in two countries, four-buck-a-gallon gas, foreclosures, and sad economic news, it felt good to make people laugh, forget their troubles for a little while. Now that the Northrup Road Players are doing so well in remembering their lines, we are seeking new venues. I thought we might have to change one word in the script if we bring the play to a school.

Fond du Lac Follies toured the new casino before the grand opening. The casino is huge and very beautiful. I saw many new machines and the upscale steak house. There are three bars in the casino and a place for non-smokers. It is amazing what $100 million buys these days.

Fond du Lac Follies jetted to Orlando. Before we get too far into this story, let me say right now that I am not a Mickey Mouse fan. It just happens that the National Council on Racism and Ethnicity convention was being held there. I was invited to be one of the featured speakers to talk about racism. I took off my moccasins at the Duluth airport, put them back on, and caught the flight to Minneapolis. I changed planes and continued on to Orlando. The Disney employees at the Disney Welcome Center welcomed us to Orlando. We were shuttled to the Disney Magical Express bus, which would take us to the Coronado Spa. Along the way, we watched a video featuring a man named Walt Disney. He looked good considering he died in 1966. We arrived at the spa and I was immediately struck by how nice everything looked. The people who worked there were friendly. I think there were two thousand people expected to attend the workshops and presentations. I was issued a badge that identified me, and it further said I was a presenter. I began meeting people, met old friends and made some new ones. When it was my time to speak, I noticed the audience had about four hundred who gathered to hear my stories. They had two of those huge TV screens on each side of me. Dr. Richard Allen of the Cherokee Nation introduced me to the crowd. He was a combat vet from the Vietnam War who served with the Marine Corps. First I introduced myself in Ojibwe to the people. I knew there were a couple of Shinnobs from Duluth who understood what I was saying. I told stories for about fifty minutes. At the end of my presentation, I told the people I hadn't mentioned the sports mascot issue yet. I told them I had one thought about it.

In a loud voice I said, "Go, Redskins!" then pointed my finger at the exit door. I added, "And take those Indians, Braves, and Chiefs with you." There was much laughter and applause as I left the stage. I went to another part of the convention center, where I signed copies of my books for about a half hour. The next morning, the bus from Disney's Magical Express carried me back to the Orlando airport. I took off my moccasins, then put them back on again. The airplane ride to Minnesota was boring and uneventful. So was the ride on the smaller airplane to Duluth.

Fond du Lac Follies motored to Morton, Motown, as I call it. The event was their annual powwow. Since my wife is a member of the Lower Sioux Indian Community, attendance was compulsory. Aaron Ezigaa drove that old silver Corvette to the doings. I know he likes driving that beautiful car. The price of gasoline was $3.99. At least we didn't have to pay four bucks for gas. My son is learning how to drive that powerful car quite well. Pat is working on her Rez and was spending her salary keeping gasoline in that gas-guzzling silver Silverado. She bought a gas-sipping car; we have personalized plates that say Bwaan (Dakota). The powwow was well attended; a lot of my wife's relatives were working there to make it a success. There was a ceremony honoring the Dow family. The highlight for me was getting to know my great-granddaughter. We just call her Baby. She is ten months old and has been walking for a month now. I never thought I would be old enough to have a great-grandchild.

The birch is peeling, so we are once again making baskets. I see that Jeff Savage and others are building a birch bark canoe again. Jeff tells me they are going to the National Museum of the American Indian to work on a wiigwaasi-jiimaan. What an honor for those Fonjalackers. My godson Zac came by with some birch bark, said he found it in a state park. So, we are making baskets. Rick Gresczyk brought a student named Colleen who wanted to learn how to work with the materials so she could make a fanning basket. We all went to the woods to gather basswood bark that we use for sewing the baskets together. Rick and the Buck knife came too close together, and he stopped bleeding after about a half hour. Every year I wonder where the baskets we make will end up.

Fond du Lac Follies motored to the Red Cliff Reservation at the invitation of Andy Gokee. Their annual Ojibwe language immersion camp was being held there. He wanted me to teach what I know about making birch bark baskets. I motored there in that beautiful, shiny '64 Corvette Sting Ray. The sun was out and the sky was blue as I drove east on Highway 13 in Wisconsin. The two-lane road hugged the south shore of Lake Superior. When driving that car, I always feel eyes on me. First, people look at the flowing lines of that forty-four-year-old sports car. Then they see me driving, and there seems to be confusion, like what is an Indian doing in that car? Then I can almost hear them say, Oh, must be a casino Indian. I arrived at the camp on Raspberry

Point and immediately began meeting people I know. Marv Defoe took time out from birch bark canoe building at the Fond du Lac to come to the immersion camp. Makes sense since he is from Red Cliff. In the morning, I watched Leonard Moose work with about twelve children in learning Ojibwemowin. In the afternoon, we took some students out to gather bark. At first Marv was apprehensive about showing me where the good birch was located on his Rez. He thought I might come back and gather some bark for the baskets I make. In the end, he decided to show me where some good trees were to be found. Marv took half of our group and I took the other half to show them what I know about removing birch from the trees. We collected enough bark for those who wanted to learn how to work with the materials. I brought willow frames and basswood bark for the stitching. It was a large group of people who wanted to learn, more than thirty initially. I got everyone started, then began answering questions about how to do it. After I taught one person how to do something, I would ask them to teach someone else what they had learned. People were at different stages of basket construction, so I stayed busy all afternoon. The next day the class size was smaller and some got real close to finishing their baskets. At the beginning I told them I couldn't guarantee they would make a basket but would guarantee they would learn how to work with the materials. I felt like I had accomplished what I set out to do, and Andy Gokee was satisfied with the teaching and learning. I think with immersion camps, language tables, college courses, schools, and ceremonies, Ojibwemowin will continue to be spoken. We will keep our language alive.

The Something Annual Veterans Powwow was held in Sawyer again at Mashkawisen. Right off the top I think Mary Northrup, our veterans service officer, and the powwow committee did an outstanding job in organizing this tribute to veterans. My wife had her food stand, called Stand Here. She passed the Rez health inspection and began churning out fry bread and tacos. Patricia also had wild rice soup for sale. Her crew consisted of my son Matthew, his woman, Jackie, her sister Cynthia and son Calvin. Aaron Ezigaa was helping by being a gopher. Tysa Goodrich, a woman from California, came to see her first powwow. My wife put her to work right away cutting up onions. There was always a line in front of Stand Here, just people buying food. Next to that stand I set up my shelter that is a combination birch bark basket sales outlet and a veterans' lounge. We had a florescent green sign that advertised Free Coffee for Veterans. One veteran was Adam, a young Marine who had been blown up in Iraq. Ray Earley, USMC Vietnam vet, told us stories about the battle of Hue City. Veterans would stop by, drink coffee, listen, and tell stories. Tysa was done with her work, so she sat in the lounge and listened to the stories. She is writing a novel about a Vietnam vet. The Rez provided gifts for their veterans. We got a leather travel bag embossed with the words Fond du Lac Ogichidaa. Inside the bag was a T-shirt, a hat, a nifty knife, a thermos, and wild rice. We sat out on the deck that sunny day and told stories and stories. Ted and I shared the Cuban Missile Crisis and a West Pac cruise where we visited Panama, Puerto Rico,

Jamaica, Japan, Okinawa, Taiwan, the Philippines, and Hong Kong. Ted said he went looking for Suzy Wong in Hong Kong but she was the wong one. Ted and I spent a bit over two years in a Marine Infantry Company. Ray and I shared the Vietnam War. By one corner of the deck there was a pile of dead bodies we had seen in the war, over there was a pile of grenade pins, C-ration cans littered the deck, and brass from fired projectiles was everywhere underfoot. Yeah, we had a good time telling stories. We are looking forward to the next liberty call. Because we are old goats, we know there are not many more times that we can gather and share stories like this.

While in Minneapolis, my wife and I were in the same place as Heid, Louise Erdrich, and Suzy, the manager at Birchbark Books. Suzy told a funny story about a man who came to the store and wanted to read a narrative written by an American Indian. She gave him a copy of one of my books. The man read for a while, then came up and told Suzy, this guy is funny. Suzy said, "He thinks he is."

Heid told us of a mural being painted on a concrete wall just a couple of blocks from the Indian Center on Franklin Avenue. We got the directions from Heid and drove to the mural site. Lisa Brown was up on a short ladder painting the white flowers that border the long, long mural. She came off her ladder and told us about the beautiful mural. The painting represents the Indians who died while living in that neighborhood. My brother Rodney Northrup died in a car accident in that area.

While looking at the mural, Pat saw Heid, Louise, and Suzy come driving up. They got out of their car, and we all stood and admired the idea of the mural, the art the artist was making, the colorful jingle dresses and ribbon shirts of the humans in the painting. The birch trees also looked good. Then we all began to have suggestions for the painter. We thought of a good title she could consider. It was Mino-bimadiziwin. I thought the painting needed a lake added somewhere. Heid thought there should be a gopher coming out of one of the drain holes of the concrete wall. I can hardly wait to see more details added to the mural.

Wayne Newton came to the Black Bear Resort's new Otter Creek Event Center. I got a postcard advising me to call for free tickets. I did, and they told me the event was sold out already. They later called back and said they had two front-row tickets for me. I don't know if I got the good tickets because I write the Follies, or because I am an elder, a veteran, a good gambler, or handsome. I asked my son Aaron Ezigaa if he wanted to go to a concert with me and said I had front-row tickets. He surprised me when he said yes. He didn't even ask who Wayne Newton was. The show was entertaining. I wanted to hear his signature song "Danke Schoen" (which would be *miigwech* in Ojibwe), but he just sang a medley of songs. He also kissed two women, told jokes, and played the electric guitar, an acoustic guitar, a banjo, and a fiddle. I was glad I went to this entertaining show. Aaron Ezigaa, age eighteen, said it was alright. I would have liked to see Wayne Newton when he was in his prime. Now he looks and sounds like an entertainer who is coming to an end of a long, successful career.

The leaves are beginning to change colors, things don't seem as green as they used to. The sky is just as bright blue as before. The nights are cooler. Ricing is here again, and members of the family at the World Headquarters of the Fond du Lac Follies have been to the Reservation lakes gathering our share of that gift from the Creator. I went into ricing feeling like a rich man because I have two big cast iron kettles and two canoes. We already had one big kettle, but my wife, Patricia, found one in an antique shop in southern Minnesota. I know we can use the second kettle to boil maple sap next spring, should be able to boil twice as fast. The new-to-us canoe was also purchased in southern Minnesota. We also have two cords of seasoned firewood. Yup, I feel like a rich man. This year we had a student who wanted to learn how to parch his rice gathered at the Sandy Lake Flowage, north of McGregor, Minnesota. I let him use my fire pit, my firewood, one of my kettles, and a canoe paddle. I showed him how to turn the rice in the kettle, how to check the parched rice so he knew it was done. I supervised him, and he learned how to turn the rice, how to keep the fire not too hot or not too cool. After two hundred pounds, I knew his life story, and he knew how to parch rice. I am just passing on what someone taught me.

I am currently working on a novel called *Dirty Copper*. It is the story of my character Luke Warmwater as a deputy sheriff in Carlton County, a big-city police officer, and finally a public defender investigator. Here is a preview from the middle of the manuscript:

Luke was driving his squad car in the northern part of the city, day shift. The radio came alive, "406," the dispatcher said.

Luke replied, "406, I'm at Tenth and Lincoln," giving his location as was the standard practice in the police department.

"406, we got a report of a purse snatching behind the hospital."

"10-4, do you have a description of the suspect?"

"406, he is a white male, long brown hair, about five foot eight, 160 pounds."

"10-4, clothing description?"

"406, no clothes, he was naked."

"Naked?"

"10-4, 406, naked."

Luke drove to the area and did a perimeter search, parked his car, and began walking through the alleys. In the second alley he saw a bare foot sticking out from behind a Dumpster. He looked and saw a white male, naked, with a brown leather purse clutched over his genitals.

Luke told him, "Stand up, drop the purse, and put your hands on the wall." The man complied, and Luke told him, "I won't search you. I can see you're unarmed. I won't ask for identification. You don't have pockets." Luke cuffed him, picked up the purse, and walked the man to the squad car. He covered the naked suspect with a blanket and radioed in to report that he had the suspect in custody and had recovered the purse.

The man in the back seat spoke up. "Wait, wait, let me tell you what happened. See, I was over in the next block. This woman had invited me over because her husband was at work. We were just getting started in the bedroom when we heard the front door being unlocked. I jumped out of bed and kicked my clothes and shoes under the bed. I escaped out the window to the fire escape. I heard heavy footsteps walking to the window. I went down the fire escape, and when I stepped off the bottom step, the fire escape went back up to the second floor. So, there I was standing in the alley wondering what to do. Then, this other naked man came running up, handed me the purse, and took off."

Luke laughed all the way to the jail. He told the desk sergeant the guy's story. It quickly spread. Some cops were saying it had happened to them.

Fond du Lac Follies has sure been jetting a lot lately. It must be because November is American Indian Heritage Month. Speaking for myself, I believe every month is American Indian Heritage Month. First I went to Dayton. To get there, I had to ride a jet to Atlanta. To get to Ohio, I had to go to Georgia first. I guess it makes some kind of airline sense to go to the Peach State to get to the Buckeye State. I proceeded to Wright State University, it was a huge place, seventeen thousand students. I met with some students who were leaders of the Native American students group. We shared some time together, and then it was time for me to tell stories and recite poetry. I stood in front of the room and told stories about the Anishinaabe and about life on the Fond du

Lac Reservation in what is now called Minnesota. I flew from Dayton to Atlanta, then on to Minneapolis and finally Duluth. I got to Sawyer and shook off the effects of jet lag. I then flew from Duluth to Minneapolis to Portland, Oregon. This event was a tribute to American veterans. American Indian veterans were honored during this event. There were quite a few people, including a Navajo code talker. His name was Samuel Sandoval, and it was interesting visiting with him. He told me to forget everything about the movie *Windtalkers*. He told me how it really was as a code talker in the Marines during World War II in the Pacific island battles. He was accompanied by his young wife; some vets asked if she was his granddaughter, but he laughed and said he was married to her. When Samuel found out I was from Minnesota, he said he was wishing for wild rice. I gave him a pound of Perch Lake rice that my family gathered last September. Also in attendance were two men who were Tuskegee Airmen. Both had flown P-51s in Europe during World War II. I was in the midst of historical figures at this event. There were quite a few American Indian veterans of the Vietnam War there also. It rained for four days and nights while I was in Portland. I thought the easiest job in Portland was being a weather forecaster. Something like, tonight we will have rain, followed by a thunderstorm tomorrow, with sprinkles in the evening and a gulley-washer storm this weekend. I only saw the bottom of the mountains because of the clouds. The rain followed me back to Minnesota. I continued shaking off the effects of jet lag.

I caught a flight to Minneapolis for a flight to Cleveland. Roberto Chavez had invited me to Cleveland

State University and NASA invited me to the John Glenn Space Center. I met some skins who worked for the space agency. At NASA, I told the employees about meeting John Herrington, the Indian astronaut. I told them I gave him a fast ride in my Corvette and asked if he wanted to drive it back. He asked if I trusted him with my sports car. I told John if NASA trusted him with a space shuttle I could trust him with my car. The employees of NASA laughed at that story. In honor of John Herrington, I took off my Marine Corps hat and wore the NASA hat he had dated and autographed. At the end of the reading, I put my NASA hat away and put my Marine Corps hat back on. I went to the airport for a flight to Detroit and caught another airplane for the trip back to Duluth. It felt good to be home.

Chapter 8

We Laughed Muchly——2009

I got the phone call all parents fear. It was my son Joe on the phone. His words sent icicles into my heart. He said, "Check on Aaron, he's been in a car crash." I called Aaron on his cellyphone. He answered and said he was in the Cloquet Hospital emergency room. I knew he was driving the '78 Monte Carlo. I also knew he was taking his finals at Fond du Lac Tribal and Community College.

I got to the hospital and asked about my son. I was directed to Room 6 of the emergency room. I walked down the hall to Room 6; my mind was swirly, full of questions. Nitam, first, I needed to see my son.

I walked into the room and saw Aaron lying on a yellow backboard. His head was immobilized. His face had streaks of dried blood, and he was still bleeding from a wound on his lower lip. It wasn't the serious kind of bleeding, the kind that spurts and squirts. Our eyes met, and I held his hand. His grip was tight, so I knew that part worked. I asked him to move his legs and he did. I thanked the Creator.

I asked him what happened. Aaron said he was going home from school on Highway 210, just past the casino. He started going up that little hill. He said he hit a stretch of black ice and slush. The car slid sideways, and he turned into the skid; the car spun and he was still sliding. He turned the steering wheel and the car slid the other way. A small pickup came over the hill and tried to stop. The truck slid and hit the passenger side of Wiwiib, his car. The impact knocked the car nose first into the ditch. He remembers getting out of the car and the arrival of the ambulance. The car Aaron was driving was T-boned.

While we were talking, Aaron's cellyphone rang. He sent a text message to a friend. I was glad to see his injuries were minor. If the truck hit him when he was sliding driver's door first, it would have been bad: major injuries or a funeral. I again thanked the Creator.

I talked to the highway patrolman. He said after looking at the car he thought Aaron used up one of his nine lives.

A group of medical people came in. They rolled him back and forth and got the backboard out from under him. Aaron said his back hurt from lying on the board. A nurse came in and cut off his shirts and began cleaning him up. When he was cleaned up, I got a closer look at the wound on his lower lip. I am not a doctor nor do I play one on TV, but that wound needed stitches. His eyelid needed a couple of stitches also.

Aaron was wheeled off for a CAT scan and X-rays. I went outside for a breath of fresh air and a smoke. I went back to Room 6 and waited. I knew my son was in good hands. I called my wife and told her the news; she was in a hospital in Saint Paul with her mother. She was torn between being with her mother or her son. She knew I was handling things on this end, so she stayed with her mom.

The doctor arrived to stitch up Aaron's wounds. While sewing, she told me the highway patrolman told her of three other incidents on that stretch of the highway that day.

Once he was sewed up, we left the emergency room. There were two young girls waiting for my son to come out. When they saw him, they hugged him and he smiled.

The next day we went to gaze at the Monte Carlo. The passenger door was pushed all the way to the driver's seat from the impact. I knew no one would ever drive that car again. The car did what it was supposed to do; it absorbed the impact and protected my son.

Aaron thought he left his laptop in the car, so he looked for it. The tow truck driver said there was no computer in the car when he towed it. Aaron gathered up his stuff from the wrecked car. I told him to go to the sheriff's office and report the theft of his computer. Aaron drove to Carlton and talked with a deputy about his missing computer. We went grocery shopping and talked about the crushed car and missing computer. We also talked about how fortunate Aaron was to escape major injuries in the car crash.

I told Aaron he got a crash course in winter driving.

This is a final salute to Chic Smith. The Marine veteran was awarded three Purple Hearts in Korea. Chic was seventy-seven years old. We will miss you at the bingo hall. Our sympathies are extended to his extended family.

Fond du Lac Follies motored to Frostbite Falls, as I call International Falls, Minnesota, to talk to three classes at the high school. The weather was the main part of this story. The thermometer read thirty below zero when I started off. The road was mostly clear except for the patches of black ice. I just puckered up when I skated across those places.

I arrived the night before I was scheduled to speak, and I became an overnight Holiday Inndian. The staff there was friendly, so if you are ever that far north it is a good place to stay. I could see Canada from the restaurant. It looked a lot like northern Minnesota. In the morning, I was worried about my car starting because it was so cold, but no problem. That Sable fired up easily in that thirty-below winter morning. The license plates on the car say Bwaan because it is my wife's car and she is Dakota.

I met the first group, an honors English class. I introduced myself in Ojibwemowin. I then asked if anyone could name an Anishinaabe author. There was a dead silence in the room until someone said Jim Northrup. I told them I always like to start with him. I named some of my favorite Anishinaabe authors starting with Margaret Noori, Louise Erdrich, Heid Erdrich, Kim Blaeser, Gerald Vizenor, and Marcie Rendon. I told the students to write down those names because there was going to be a quiz the next time I came through Frostbite Falls. The students had watched the video *Jim Northrup: With Reservations* before I came to the classroom. The final credits were rolling as I walked in. The students got to see me in person after watching the half-hour video.

I recited some poems that weren't in the video, told them boarding school stories and some war stories from the Vietnam War. I finished by telling my dog stories. Tom Vollum whisked me off to the next class, which was Anishinaabeg students. I stood up and told similar stories to these students. I allowed time for questions they might have about me or my writing. One of the students asked how long it took to write a short story, a poem. I told them, from the beginning all the way to the end. I told them I don't keep track of the time because I am so busy keeping track of the story or poem. I stressed the importance of rewriting and revising. I thought that was a thought-provoking thought from a tenth-grade student.

The third class was very much like the second and even had a lot of the same faces in it. Tom Vollum did a good job of putting together the doings, and I saw him weilding a spoon during the afternoon feast. I told a few stories to the family and students that gathered as a way of singing for my supper. I will long remember my friendly visit to Frostbite Falls.

Fond du Lac Follies motored to the Black Bear Casino for the first ever State of the Band Address by Karen Diver and the rest of the Reservation Business Committee. The important things I learned were that our per capita payment will continue and that no one would be laid off. I left the meeting and I was smiling just hard.

I like winter, and this one has been especially good. We have had enough snow and the below-zero weather to make it a good winter. I really like it when the sun sprinkles sparkling diamonds in the snow in my back-yard. I am getting old so I don't spend as much time outside as I used to. I enjoyed downhill skiing and trudging through the deep snow on snowshoes. I have fond memories of teaching my grandsons how to build a fire in the deep snow. I like seeing the sun getting higher in the sky because that means sugar bush is coming. I will spend more time outside then.

Fond du Lac Follies motored to the Black Bear Casino for a meal we had been drooling about. We were going to the Seven Fires Steak House. We previously had over-eaten at the buffet and eaten at the Sage Deli during a bingo game. We had to see if our favorite machines were giving away money first. I fought one to a stand-still when I broke even. I was glad too because I could really use the money. My wife found a machine that was giving away money so I became a cheerleader. I saw my sister Nita walking toward the exit, swearing under and over her breath at the machine she had been playing. I invited her to eat with us, so she stuck around and we cheered Pat's slot machine on. Pat cashed out when she had quadrupled her money.

We walked through the fancy glass doors and immediately hit a brick wall of ambience. This was without a doubt an upscale place to eat. The flowers on each table, the candles, and the quiet put us in the mood for a special dining experience. We were given menus roughly the size of a dikinaagan, a cradleboard, and were shown to our seats. I struggled to unfold my napkin that was folded in an intricate shape. It was a thick cloth napkin about the size of a bath towel. Pat and Nita had a seafood appetizer, and I ordered a Moosehead beer; instead of chugging from the bottle, I was given a tall, skinny, frosted glass to sip my beer from. Classy. The time to order came. Nita wanted the walleye, Pat wanted the filet mignon, and I wanted the twenty-ounce rib eye steak. The waitperson took our order, and I thought I was related to her, so she told us who her parents were. With that information I was able to tell her that her dad's gramma and my gramma were sisters, yup, cousins.

The food arrived, and we began to eat. The taste of the food told me the Rez got their money's worth when they did the nationwide search for the chef. Pat said her food was cooked exactly as she liked it. Nita had a hunk of walleye that was almost Frisbee size. The taste of my food was beyond description. I quit talking at this point and just cut and chewed, cut and chewed. We finished and left in a food haze. I felt like I wouldn't have to eat for two days, and I didn't. Imagine. . . food that good in a place owned by us just eight miles down the road.

Question: What do you want inscribed on your tombstone?
Answer: Don't stand there gawking. Go get a shovel.

Kenny Rogers came to the Black Bear Casino to do a show. I saw his big green, unmarked, tour bus parked in front of the hotel. I have long been a fan of Kenny since his days with the First Edition. I suppose I could sing along with at least six or seven of his songs. I went to the concert with Ray Earley, his wife, Cheryl, and my son Matthew and his significant other, Jackie. The Otter Creek Entertainment Center was overflowing with fans. We were seated near the back, almost by the Barnum ZIP code. Fortunately they had Jumbotron screens, and we were able to see quite nicely. The sound quality was great.

Kenny sang and sang, "Ruby," "Coward of the County," "The Gambler," and more. The opening chords told us what song was coming next. We sang along with them, heads nodding, shoulders swaying. In between one series of songs, Kenny showed pictures of his twin sons, age four and a half. The women in the crowd oohed and aahed when the pictures came up.

In between another series of songs, Kenny showcased his fiddle player, said she was the best in the world. I only caught her first name—Amy—don't know if he threw out her last name. She played good music. Toward the end, Kenny Roges sang "Lady." I thoroughly enjoyed the concert. It was certainly worth every penny I paid for the tickets. I didn't pay any pennies for the tickets.

I am waiting to hear the crows, which tells me it is time to tap maple trees for our sugar bush. I can see the warm sun has already melted the little circle of snow around the base of the trunks. I had to carve some more taps.

My son Aaron and I cut, drilled, and carved the maple sticks we use. I like using wood taps because they swell when they get wet so we don't lose any sap down the trunk. Our goal is two hundred taps.

It may be just my memory, but winter always takes a couple of our elders. My mother-in-law Geraldine Dow died recently. She lived a long life full of helping other people. She just helped people because it was the way she was raised. Some she helped by listening, and no one ever walked away from her table empty. She fed any and all that came to visit. I have a couple of fond memories I will share about this remarkable woman.

I remember hearing the story about when she was a little girl playing with her cousins. The Pipestone bus came, and she got on with them. She was four years old. Her parents found her at the boarding school. In the early 1940s, while her husband, Howard, was driving tanks for General Patton, Gerry took a job as Rosie the Riveter in Seattle, working in a shipyard. She contributed to the war effort. Howard and Gerry raised their family at the Lower Sioux Community. They later moved to Saint Paul so he could find work. Visiting Indians could always find a meal or a place to sleep at their home.

When I was courting their oldest daughter, Patty, I paid the bride-price by giving Gerry two and a half horses. She smiled and said, I was thinking of getting a lawnmower, and now I have one. When I left her house, my belly was full.

We shall long remember this exceptional woman.

My younger sister Doris Ann also died recently. She was sixty-one. It is hard for me to write about my sister and friend. She was always quick to offer a cup of coffee or a meal or an ear when I visited her. She told the funniest stories. Doris was born on February 14, so every Valentine's Day I sang her our traditional family song that goes, "Happy birthday to you, happy birthday to you, you belong in a zoo, you belong in a zoo, you look like an animal, and you smell like one, too."

She moved back to the Rez from the Cities in the early '90s. I was glad because it was easier to visit her on Mahnomen Road. She was called Doe, the Mayor of Mahnomen. Lee Staples did the ceremony that helped send Doris to the other side to meet her relatives who had passed on before her.

The Sawyer Community Center was where her funeral was held. The fire was burning outside. There were quite a few of her friends and relatives who came together to help send her off. Her children and grandchildren were seated on one side of the aisle. Doris Ann's brothers and sisters were seated on the other side of the aisle. We were seated in our birth order. Empty chairs were used to signify other brothers or sisters who had passed on.

During the ceremony, in Ojbwe, Lee Staples told Doris what she would see on her four-day journey to the other side. We ate and smoked with Doris. The non-smokers took their tobacco outside and placed it in the fire. After the casket was closed for the final time, Lee explained what he had said in English to us. We left knowing what to expect when our time comes.

Doris, every Valentine's Day I will sing to you, "Happy birthday to you, happy birthday to you, you belong in a zoo, you belong in a zoo. . ."

My sons and I went out to tap maple trees. The crew consisted of my son Matthew, his SO Jackie, sons Joseph and Aaron Ezigaa. We drilled 194 holes after offering tobacco. Two bald eagles circled us while we were tapping trees. We know they will carry the message to the Creator that some Shinnobs are still using the gift of maple sap.

I supervised from my lawn chair placed on the logging road. I pointed where I wanted them to drill, tap, and place a milk jug. We collected our sap and brought it home to the fire pit and sugar camp in the yard.

We hung one kettle and began to boil. We filtered the sap as we poured it into the kettle. The snow began falling in huge flakes as the kettle began to steam. We boiled and kept adding sap to the kettle. Dr. Vainio, his wife, Ivy, and son, Jacob, came to see how we make maple syrup. We explained that this was our first boil. The next time they visit we will put them to work. We Tom Sawyered people in Sawyer. Patricia and her sister Cynthia pulled in from the Lower Sioux Community. They were just in time to do the finish boiling and canning of the syrup.

May is always one my favorite times of the year. It is when we go to the sugar bush to make maple syrup. For almost twenty years I have been writing about going to the sugar bush, and I worry sometimes that I will repeat myself.

The basics are the same: the snow, the sun, and the quiet of the woods. Also the trees, the kettle, the firewood, the drill, the taps. I guess the only real difference is who will visit. There were two cords of seasoned firewood waiting, two kettles, and 192 new milk jugs from a Duluth dairy. We were ready. I had a good, well-trained crew. It was my sons, Jim, Matthew, Joe, Aaron Ezigaa, and Calvin. Also my nephew Kris and daughter-in-law Jackie. My part was easy; all I did was sit and lip point at what I wanted done next. At the end of the day my lips were just tired.

Question: What do you call a Shinnob with no lips?
Answer: Pointless.

This year I once again told them about being careful not to spill any sap because it comes out of the trees one drop at a time. We went to the woods and began to drill the trees and insert a tap into the holes. I parked my lawn chair in the middle of the logging road and simply pointed out what I wanted done. Two bald eagles flew over us as we moved through the woods. It took just one day to drill the 192 holes, tap the taps in, and hang milk jugs. We had a good run of sap for a couple of days, then the sap froze up. For seven days, the temperature didn't rise above thirty degrees. We did boil down our first run of sap. Once again I was telling my crew what to do; I had taken to calling them my minions. My son Aaron asked if I could move my chair and supervise from "way the hell over there," out of the way. I complied.

Bill Howes, a Fonjalacker, brought some students from Saint Scholastica to the sugar bush to see how we were doing things. I think the students learned the way we do things around this fire.

Friends from Michigan won the award for traveling the farthest to visit our sugar bush. Janis Fairbanks, her husband, Caz, and Mike Zimmerman came from southern Michigan to see the magic of our sugar bush. Al Everywhere Hunter, Sandra Indian, and two grandsons won the international award for traveling here from Canadia to see our sugar bush. Anishaa, I was just jiving about the awards. We don't give out awards, only knowledge. We had a Flambonian, Lenelle Hrabik, from Lac du Flambeau, who came to help us work. Finally, Jana Hollingsworth and Clint Austin came from the *Duluth News Tribune* to write a story and take pictures of our method of making syrup from maple sap.

My minions worked well together; they laughed and joked the whole way through. Once when Kris was splitting wood, Matthew told him, if you're going to hit that wood like a girl, hit it like a big girl, at least. Once it was sweet enough outside, we brought it inside where my wife further boiled it, filtered it, and canned it for storage.

Question: What if the pope came to the sugar bush?
Answer: Holy See, we'd have papal maple syrupal.

The end of the sugar bush season also means the beginning of the Corvette season. I wake that beautiful car from hibernation when the state quits salting the roads. The body of the Sting Ray is fiberglass, but the guts underneath are all steel so it would rust after a couple of Minnesota winters. I charged the battery, sneezed into the tires, added fresh gas, and that big V-8 rumbled to life when I turned the key.

Immediately I took that car on the county road south of Sawyer that has a series of five ninety-degree turns. When we went around the corners, I leaned, but that car stayed rock steady all the way through each turn.

Already I am wondering where that car and I will motor to this year. I am also wondering what I will have to repair or replace on the forty-five-year-old car. My wife is afraid to drive that car because it is too fast, too low, and too powerful, so I have to drive it. Oh, the sacrifices I make for my family.

Question: What do you say when visitors leave your house?
Answer: Giga-waabaabaabye. (Ojibberish)

Fond du Lac Follies motored to Gakaabikaang to meet with Rick Gresczyk's class at Metro State. I arrived in time to see students carrying food toward the classroom.

I was just in time for a feast—what timing, eh? Rick made an Ojibwe prayer for the food, included some tobacco.

This was a culturally diverse group. I ate wild rice and food from Somalia. I told stories for a while, maybe a bit more than an hour. The students seemed to enjoy my presentation; they laughed at the appropriate times, were quietly thinking during other parts.

After I was done, I headed north to the quiet of the Rez. I just couldn't stand being in the city any longer. There is too much of everything. I drove north to the welcoming dark of the northern Minnesota night.

Fond du Lac will have its first language immersion camp this summer. The location is the Reservation's campground on the north end of Big Lake, in Sawyer. We attended an RBC meeting and during the new business part of the meeting, I spoke about our plans for the camp.

My son Jim will show how he builds a waagi-nogaan, maybe two. We can use those for shelter for the three days of the camp. I told the RBC how we would have stations where various artists make birch bark baskets, black ash baskets, moccasins, fry bread. One station would be a cribbage game where people could learn how to count in Ojibwe. We would like to have fluent speakers traveling from station to station explaining in Ojibwe what each artist is doing.

We are calling this effort the First Annual Fond du Lac Reservation Ojibwe Language Camp. Everyone is welcome at our camp.

Dr. Margaret Noori of the University of Michigan brought ten students to the World Headquarters of the Fond du Lac Follies. Megan also brought Asmat and daughters Shannon and Fionna. Two other teachers completed the group—Howard Kimewon and Pat Osawamick were from Wikwemikong, an unceded First Nation in Canada. We met at the Black Bear Casino, where we ate together in the buffet. We went home, and they went gambling. The next morning the whole group came to Sawyer in three vans. The sixteen people wanted to taste our maple syrup, so they made French toast, also bacon and eggs.

I was making awls for the upcoming birch season where we sew baskets. The table held maple sticks, nails, glue, and my Buck carving knife. I had completed niizh by the time the college students finished eating; bezhig goal was to make ishwaaswi awls altogether. There were nanaan chairs in a circle on the deck. Zhaangaachiwag wanted to learn how to make an awl, so I showed them what I do. It was sunny outside, but I knew the thermometer read zero, gaawiin gegoo, not too many weeks ago. I had zero degrees, and I looked all over for some, looked under the couch, in the bathroom, in the tool-shed. I could find no degrees anywhere.

I showed them the process I used. I stood bezhig maple stick on end and drove a nail in the center using my hammer. I pulled it out and pounded it back in a little deeper. I pulled the nail and put glue on half of it. I then used niishwaaswi strokes to set the nail at the desired depth. I then used my grinder using the niizh wheels. I would grind a bit then cool the nail. I ground the heads off of niiwin nails, kept them cool while grinding. The Michigan students were happy with the awls they had made. The awls were a tool, and they learned how to make another if they wanted too.

I gave them a naanimidana miskwaabikoons (fifty-cent) tour of the Rez. We went to the Sawyer Center, where my sister Nita Fineday showed them around. A visit to Perch Lake. I talked about wild rice. The Rez museum was next followed by a drive-by visit to the Mino-ayaawin clinic. The students were full of questions as we circled back to Sawyer. I think they will long remember their visit to the World Headquarters of the Fond du Lac Follies. I wrote down their names in case there is a quiz.

The Corvette is in the shop, needs yet another transmission. After two times, I think I need a heavy-duty transmission, the kind used in race cars. I like to think the Corvette and I are the antidote to global warming because we are so cool together. Being cool costs money.

The planning paid off and the First Annual Nagaaji-wanaang Fond du Lac Ambe Ojibwemodaa language camp was excellent. My son Aaron and godson Zac built one waaginogan for shelter from the rain and sun. My son Jim built the second one. At least a dozen campers joined in building the teaching lodge. The camp was held on the north end of Big Lake, in Sawyer. We could see eagles flying over the doings.

Patricia put up her food structure and fed the multitudes three meals a day. One camper said he wouldn't come back next year if Pat wasn't the cook. She smiled at the compliment. Veronica Smith and Marky Dwyer worked with her. Some of the campers shared their food and helped out with the cooking.

The idea of having a language camp started over a game of Scrabble. Rick Gresczyk, Patricia, and I played the game late into the night. We talked about the need for a camp, but the hard part was selecting the dates to hold the camp. Once we decided, Rick recruited fluent Ojibwe speakers. Gordon Jourdain of Lac La Croix, Nancy Jones of Ontario and her son Dan Jones. Randy Gresczyk came to help our camp. When Nancy Jones heard about the camp, she wanted to attend. She likes teaching Ojibwemowin and taught campers how to make fry bread on a stick over an open fire, among other things. Dennis Jones stopped by for a visit, as did David Niib Aubid. We were rich with fluent speakers.

I asked the Reservation Business Committee for assistance and they agreed to give the fluent speakers a stipend. The RBC asked various divisions of the tribal government to help. Rez Department of Natural Resources provided canoes to be used in the canoe race; the game wardens came to be the safety boat during the race. The library gave plates, cups, and bowls for the campers to use. The support from the Rez was very much appreciated.

Campers began arriving Sunday evening. On Monday we registered 84 humans; on Tuesday it was

144, and Wednesday we had 43. I think the canoe races thrilled a lot of folks. There were seven canoes. My son Matthew coordinated the race and set out his buoys. We laughed muchly in Ojibwemowin. As for me, I showed the campers how to work with birch bark, basswood, and green willow to make a basket. It was good to have the camp when the birch bark was peeling easily. Rick Gresczyk taught campers how to sing songs in Ojibwemowin. He also organized the games. One game was Simon says; the game was played using Ojibwemowin commands.

The media was there, Channel 6, the Duluth newspaper, and an indie film crew. The filmmakers are going to make a ten-minute documentary and present it to the RBC. Three RBC members joined us during the talking circle in one of the teaching lodges. Chairwoman Karen Diver, Wally Dupuis, and Sandy Shabiash spoke a few words. I felt proud when Sandy, the Sawyer representative, introduced herself in Ojibwemowin. Randy Gresczyk brought out his drum, and the RBC members joined us in circling the singers.

At the talking circle, some of the campers talked about what the experience meant to them. The positive comments far outweighed the negative ones. One negative comment was that the event was too short. Another one was that we could have gotten the information out earlier. Some campers said it was such a nice spot to hold the camp. Others were glad it was a family event. The laughter of the children could be heard almost constantly as they played on the swings. It felt good to hear children teaching each other how to pronounce new words. Another comment was made about how everyone was made to feel welcome at the doings. Others wanted to know how they could help next year.

After the camp ended, the campers formed a long line and walked through the campground picking up trash. We also talked about planning for the second annual language camp here in Sawyer. One suggestion was to have the campers bring their own cups, plates, and bowls so we can cut down on the use of Styrofoam. The planning for the second annual Ojibwemowin camp has begun. We learned and will make it better next year.

Well, we did it. The Follies has been appearing in print for twenty years with this issue. I was going to quit writing the Follies after that length of time, but my wife said go for twenty-five, and I said okay. So, let us all gather around and sing the traditional song. All together now. . .

Happy birthday to it
Happy birthday to it
Happy birthday dear Follies
Happy birthday to it.

There. Done with that for another year. And what a different world we live in now compared to August 1989.

I was forty-six then, and since I began studying the Ojibwe language, I can now say with great confidence niizhwaasimidana ashi ingodwaaswi endaso biboonigiz. I was forty-six when I started writing the Follies. The Fond du Lac Follies has been in print niizhtana ashi niizh daso biboonagad.

Twenty years. That is a lot of Rez Cars and dogs ago. In that time period we have made more than a thousand birch bark fanning baskets, hundreds of gallons of maple syrup, and tons of wild rice and went to too damn many funerals.

Three of my books have been published, and I have written and performed in two plays.

We have traveled quite a bit also. We went to England and Scotland in '95. I went to Norway twice in '97. We have been to Canada twice, once in '91 and again in '92, and Mexico in '94, specifically Mexico City. I was in Amsterdam in '97, and that is all I am going to say about that.

I have visited more than fifty reservations or pueblos. We also visited great cities of the United States, even Disney World, in Orlando. I didn't go on any of the rides or look for Mickey or Minnie.

I am reminded of a quote by Winston Churchill, the Englishman who helped win World War II. "We must take change by the hand or rest assuredly; change will take us by the throat."

Change is everywhere, even in the Follies. When I first starting writing it, the length was one thousand words; now it is a sleek eight hundred words.

The Fond du Lac Veterans Powwow was held in Sawyer. It felt good to be honored for choices we made when we were young. Chuck Smith, USMC, Fond du Lac's veterans service officer, has done a great job of organizing the honoring of Reservation and visiting veterans.

My wife set up her food stand called Stand Here and I set up the basket factory/veterans' lounge next door. The only part that was missing was Ray Earley, USMC vet, who faithfully attends this event. He had a good reason for missing the festivities; he was in the VA hospital. He is now out of the hospital but felt bad that he missed everything in Sawyer. I snagged him a T-shirt from the event.

I think this was the largest powwow we ever had for veterans. I later heard they had 45 drums and 845 dancers. It felt good to be honored by the Reservation and the people at the powwow.

We got a dog for this house on Northrup Road. He is a full-blooded but not enrolled dachsund. He is now called Oscar Mayer wiener dog. I have observed that there is a lot of dog between his front and rear legs. His short legs carry him rapidly around the house. His little paws make pitter-patter noises as he dashes about. He is becoming adept at avoiding the big human feet as he runs around. Oscar likes to cuddle. We give him commands in Ojibwemowin, and he is learning Ojibwemowin. Patricia took him for a visit to see his maw. He tried to nurse but she wouldn't let him. He was content to sleep next to her all night long. Oscar came home and it felt good to hear his little feet running around the house. With our history with dogs, we are wondering how long he will be here.

Fond du Lac Follies motored to the Red Cliff Reservation for their annual language camp. Andy Gokee invited us to come and teach birch bark basket making with the campers. Patricia and I motored along the south shore of Lake Superior in her Mercury Sable, which wears license plates that say Bwaan. It was just a short jaunt, a bit more than a hundred miles, and was a scenic drive along Highway 13. I didn't take the Corvette because it was in the garage (again, we suspected a bad head gasket).

We began meeting campers and people from last year's language camp. We sat around and immersed ourselves in English conversation. I told the campers I couldn't guarantee they would make a basket, but I could guarantee they would learn how to work with hand tools and the materials we use to make baskets. There are some people who haven't worked with hand tools much; I am glad we didn't have any skin punctures. We went to the woods to gather birch bark. There is a nice stand of birch less than two miles from the campground.

After we were done for the day, we stopped at the Isle Vista Casino. We gambled a bit, then decided to eat. At one end of the room we saw a birch bark canoe. I thought, this can only be one of those beautiful canoes made by Marv Defoe. I felt good that his reservation was honoring him by displaying one of his creations.

We looked closer at the canoe and discovered the casino had turned Marv's canoe into a salad bar. What? A salad bar complete with a glass sneeze shield was the top of that beautiful canoe. Somehow it didn't look or feel right. It seemed almost sacrilegious to me.

The next day at the language camp, we talked to Marv and told him we saw one of his canoes. Then I showed him a picture of the salad bar. I told him about my feelings about how they used his canoe. He agreed with me. I heard later he was elected to their tribal council, and one of his first acts was to remove the salad bar from wiigwaas jiiman.

Fond du Lac Follies motored to the Black Bear Casino to see the Hells Angels. I had seen the Hells Angels once before, in the early 1960s. I was a young Marine military policeman stationed at Barstow, California. The freeway wasn't completed yet, and the main highway ran through the middle of the base. I was directing traffic at the front gate, and I was standing on a half barrel in the middle of the intersection. The barrel was painted yellow and red and had reflectors attached. I stopped the cross-traffic when I began to hear a lot of motorcycles coming.

The Hells Angels came down the off-ramp and came toward me, must have been at least fifty of them. They came to the front gate, and I waved them through. When they were going through the gate, some of them decided to weave on both sides of my barrel. I just stood up there waving as they went roaring by. And that was the first time I had seen the Hells Angels up close.

As I got close to the Black Bear Casino I was looking for the familiar black leather jackets with their colors. I was disappointed because all I saw were cops. I had read the newspaper and knew the officers were prepared for the five-day visit of the Hells Angels to our area. The Hells Angels had rented the Lost Isle Bar for their get-together. About two hundred of them had rented rooms in the Black Bear Casino and Hotel, I later learned.

The police were in the hotel and were scattered around the parking lot and some were parked out on Highway 210. There was a helicopter flying low, circling, apparently keeping an eye on the Hells Angels. There were police inside the casino following the Hells Angels around. Ferd Martineau, Fond du Lac's secretary-treasurer, asked the police to leave the casino because they were interfering with the casino customers, Hells Angles and otherwise. The police complied.

Next, chair Karen Diver asked the police to leave the Black Bear Casino property. She told them they would be called if necessary. I watched her walk around the casino handing out playing cards to the Hells Angels. She said she wanted them to feel welcome at the Fond du Lac Reservation. Most of the Hells Angels took the gifts.

I found the Hells Angels were courteous as I talked with them in the casino. One even held the door for me as he walked through ahead of me.

I drove near the Lost Isle Bar, and I could see many squad cars of different colors and different jurisdictions parked in a rough perimeter around the gathering site of the Hells Angels. I saw a military Black Hawk helicopter rotating between the casino and the bar.

I talked with two small-business owners in the area and asked how business was after the five hundred Hells Angels had departed. Both reported their sales were down; even regular customers were staying away because of the large number of police in the area.

Later I learned the law enforcement costs for police overtime was $185,000.

Question: What are some differences between the Hells
     Angels and the police?
Answer: Guns and budgets, and that whole law and
     order thing.

Fond du Lac Follies motored to the Ditchbanks area of
the Rez to check on water levels in some of the wild rice
lakes. Charles Nahganub was my local Indian guide on
this venture into the wilds of the Rez. Charlie works for
the Rez Department of Natural Resources.

    We drove to four sites around the Rez and measured
the water level, then recorded the depths in a logbook.
Charlie said the numbers would be crunched back at the
office using a software program.

    I am glad to know someone is watching the water
levels in the Rez water systems to ensure we have good
water levels for wild rice.

    One day while I was visiting with Charlie at the
kitchen table, he suggested saying *manoomin* instead of
wild rice. I liked the idea so much I have decided not to
use those words anymore, unless I am talking about that
black paddy rice peddled all over Minnesota highways.

    Longtime readers of the Follies might remember
when I banned a word from my vocabulary before. It
was seventeen years ago when I gave the word *Indian* a
break. I quit saying the word for a year because of that
Christopher Columbus nonsense. This is the same idea,
remove *wild rice* from my speech and writing. This time,

however, I won't give my sons a dollar every time I slip up and say *wild rice*. Instead of making rice I will make *manoominike*. The paddy rice makers can keep those old words—*wild rice*—for their product. I shall use the older word *manoomin* for that plant that we turn into food.

My son Jim and I went to Dead Fish Lake to manoominike. The Rez had decided to open this particular lake for elders only. The notice said people would be admitted to the lake on a first-come, first-served basis. According to the rules, manoominike would begin at 1000. We wanted to be able to use that lake, so we planned to be standing tall on the lakeshore at 0700.

We left the house at 0730, after packing and loading the tobacco, canoe, lunch, coffee, water, and knockers on the truck. We headed for the lake. I was doing my mental checklist when, oops, we had forgotten the pole. I turned the truck around and went home to get the pole. Then we headed for the lake.

Tysa Goodrich followed. She is writing a novel and one of her characters goes to the lake for manoomin. She didn't know anything about manoomin so she flew in from California to do her research. She came to the Rez a couple days early, so we put her to work splitting and stacking firewood. I told her there was more to manoominike than just gliding around in a canoe. She was apprehensive about hitting her foot with the ax, but after she conquered her fears she was able to split a log after many whacks. She was better at stacking than splitting.

We drove to the lake hoping to be the first to sign

up. When we got there, I discovered nitaawisag Rick Defoe and Leo Peterson were already there, apparently they didn't have to go back home for a pole.

Jim and I began visiting with our cousins. I signed up with the Rez game wardens and noticed the dew was burning off the lake as the sun got stronger. Tysa looked out at the growing manoomin and wanted to know where the lake was located. Using his lips, Jim pointed it out to her; she thought the manoomin was a field of grass.

We put our canoe in the lake and loaded the tools. In looking around the lake I remembered back to all my relatives who had gathered here for manoominike. I looked over to the north side of the lake and remembered my grandfather grew up there more than a hundred years ago. I was connected to those generations. Other Shinnobs from Fond du Lac began arriving and signing up with the game wardens. Laughing and visiting broke out immediately. People were helping others take the canoes off the cars and trucks. We harvested manoomin. We brought it home and spread it out in the sun. We fired up the big cast iron kettle and parched our manoomin.

After the first day of the harvest, I got some numbers from Charlie. Seventy-five canoes went out on the first day. The Rez bought 10,600 pounds of manoomin. Five canoes didn't sell their rice to the Rez. We are rare.

Fond du Lac Follies motored to LCO Tribal College in Hayward, Wisconsin. I had been invited there because the Indian literature class was using my first book,

Walking the Rez Road, in their studies. What an honor, I thought; someone cared enough about my writing to actually study how I use words to tell my stories.

It has been several years since I last visited LCO Tribal College, and I could see the changes because of the new buildings. I stopped in the library for directions and could see how that part of the college had improved. I also noticed how cheerful the people were. The students and some faculty members were a good audience when I read and recited poetry. They asked many astute questions at the end of my presentation. I asked the students if they could name any Anishinaabe authors. It was quiet for a while until one student began naming ten of them. I led the applause for her.

Of course, I motored there in the '64 Corvette. It looked like one of my last runs before the salted roads shut me down for the year. The big motor roared a song to my ears all the way there and back.

Oscar Mayer Weiner Dog brings smiles to the faces that live here and the human faces that visit. He eats good, puppy food only. As a result he is growing, but this is an unusual dog: he doesn't grow up, he grows longer. I think he is tall as he is going to be, but I don't know how long he will grow. I have never had a dog that grows horizontally and not vertically.

Oscar understands the Ojibwemowin words *ambe*, *omaa*, *agwajiing*, *nibaan*, *gego*, and *bizaan*, and we are working on *bekaa*. Oscar Mayer, Meyer (spelling varies) Weiner Dog goes through the same routine every time he comes in the house. It is the same whether he has been outside ten minutes or two hours. He runs around in circles rapidly, making squealing noises as if he is happy to be inside. He jumps up into the easy chair, then jumps down. Along the way he picks up one of his chew toys and continues running around. His feet noises sounds like a big German shepherd. The routine ends when he jumps up on an easy chair to sleep.

My wife reports that so far he has chewed up four pairs of shoes and two pairs of slippers. He especially likes brain-tanned deer hides. We hope he doesn't end up as a Great Horned Owl Happy Meal.

I have watched some television sports lately. One thing I have noticed is how many baseball and football players and coaches spit on the ground. Ish.

When I was growing up, tuberculosis hit the Indian community hard. If you went to just about any house you could find someone in bed suffering from the disease, or maybe they were away at a TB san, sometimes for years of bed rest or medicines. My dad, Bope, lost half a lung to the disease at the san called Nopeming near Duluth.

My sister Judy and I went to the one at Walker, Minnesota, called Agwajiing. I was probably about four years old, young enough to be sleeping in a big crib. As I recall, my therapy consisted of playing in a sandbox outside in the sun. One of the harshest rules in the san was no spitting; another was to cover coughs and sneezes. Some sixty years later, I still follow those rules.

So, what message are these professional athletes giving us? It is okay to spit on the ground, nookomisinaanig, if you are on TV? One would think they would be more careful in these days of flu, swine flu, and other airborne diseases. I wouldn't want to be the guy who has to clean the bull pen or sidelines after these guys have been spitting for a couple of hours. Ish.

The Fond du Lac Reservation once again honored their military veterans. The setting for this gala event was the Black Bear Casino's Otter Creek Entertainment Center. Chuck Smith, USMC, should get credit for organizing and coordinating this event. I am sure Mary Northrup, US Army, our former veterans service officer, should get some of the credit also.

The Reservation's honor guard performed their duties with honor. I thought of listing their names but would probably get the spelling wrong on some of them, so I'll just say, thanks guys and gals, see you at the next funeral.

The Cedar Creek Singers should be thanked for bringing their drum and songs to the honoring. Their rendition of "A Veteran's Song" thrills me every time I hear it.

Robert Sonny Peacock, US Navy Vietnam veteran, told some revealing and emotional stories about his time in the war. He is the former chairman of the Reservation Business Committee and currently president of the Fond du Lac Tribal College. Sonny was a Corpsman.

After the talk-talk was done, we ate a meal catered by the Black Bear Casino. The old veterans merely stayed in their chairs as young people jumped up to get the meals and deliver them. The prime rib was delicious; I had to have seconds on that part of the meal.

After the chewing was mostly done, Chuck Smith asked the Vietnam veterans to identify themselves by standing up. I did a quick estimate and saw between twenty and twenty-five veterans standing tall.

He called each one by name, and one of his workers delivered a package that contained manoomin (sage), a Rez pin, and a beautiful, personalized embroidered jacket. In bright yellow and red the front of the jacket says Ogichidaa, Fond du Lac, Jim, and US Marines. On the back of the jacket it says Marines, Viet Nam Vet. There is the familiar Rez logo in the center. The jacket is made of black wool with leather sleeves and knitted cuffs.

At the risk of looking a gift jacket in the mouth, mine had a sort of stayed-in-the-warehouse-too-long musty smell to it. No problem. I just hung mine outside in the good cleansing Sawyer air for a couple days. I am proud to wear that jacket. But, I still believe we must stop making veterans.

Chapter 9

Wife for Life Patricia—2010

Shinnob Jep, the play, will be performed at the Otter Creek Event Center at the Black Bear Casino. The date of the production will be January 16, 2010. The Northrup Road Players will do the play once again. Matthew Northrup will reprise his role of Franklin Lake, Jackie Busker will once again be Tradish Ikwe, and Eddie LaFave will be John Johnson Jr. I shall be Al. In the past, the Northrup Road Players have performed the play at the Weisman Art Museum in Minneapolis, the Mille Lacs Reservation, the Lac du Flambeau Reservation, three locations within the Fond du Lac Reservation, and once at an Anishinaabe language conference in Duluth, Minnesota.

Question: Are you overweight?
Answer: No, I am underheight.

When we staged *Shinnob Jep*, according to casino management they had 1,250 tickets out. I don't know how many ticket holders actually showed up. The first time

I tried counting I lost track at 679, the second time was around 757. I asked the actors from the Northrup Road Players if they had counted. In unison they said nah. I quit counting and went back to thinking about doing the best we could with *Shinnob Jep*.

We had rehearsed for ten straight days, and we knew our lines. We practiced saying the lines in different ways. We rehearsed twice on the day of the performance.

Being good actors, we checked our props; everything was ready. I gave a copy of the script so the light and sound people could follow along. We were each fitted with mobile microphones. We did a sound check and it was good. The Cedar Creek Singers were ready, drumsticks poised. Their song would open the play. The actors were in their places. My place was along the wall, in the audience. I wanted to walk through the audience greeting my relatives and friends, and just a general hi, how are ya, hi, how are ya to the ones I didn't know.

While I was waiting, twenty minutes before I started walking up on the stage, Rocky, he of casino management, asked me if I would change the script. He asked if I could remove the swear word in the play. I told him I gave them the script two years ago, and they could have objected to the use of a swear word. But not twenty minutes before I was to start. I said no. I based my answer on artistic freedom and freedom of speech as stated in the Indian Civil Rights Act (1968).

Rocky asked me to think of the children in the audience. I told him some of them were my grandchildren. I further thought this was an Indian casino evening show; we weren't doing an after-school special or Sunday school. I told him I wouldn't change the script.

Oddly, he didn't object to the use of the word *wiinag* as a character's name in the script or Boogids wild rice tools in the commercials.

I walked up on stage and began the play. Like any game-show host, I had to have a lovely assistant. I chose Patricia to come help; she marked off the questions on the flip chart and kept track of the winnings. She also was the judge on the powwow questions.

I looked at the audience. I thought it was an equal mix of Chimooks and Shinnobs.

As we came to the offending line, my son Matthew heard them click his microphone off; he said later he just spoke louder, much louder. If they had read the script a little deeper, they would have seen where I repeat his answer. They didn't turn my microphone off, but I still hate censorship.

The audience liked my show. I heard much laughter. When people are laughing, they are not thinking about the Iraq, Afghan, Pakistan war, not thinking about the expected layoff at work, the rising cost of gasoline. They are just laughing. As I waited for the laughter to die down, I was thinking . . . Was it something I said? I sure hope so.

The play went on all the way to the end. We bowed and accepted the applause. Then the lights went out, and it was over. The Cedar Creek Singers sang a traveling song.

As I walked off the stage, I was thinking of that famous show business quote, "You'll never work in this town again."

As we sat in the casino, we talked about the play. Some people walking by said the found it interesting and educational. One other person said we were funny. One old lady, I think she was from Mille Lacs, said she had to tell her friends what *wiinag* meant. We basked in the adoration. Those praises made up for all of the hours we spent rehearsing.

———————————————

Question: What do you call an Indian with a college degree?

Answer: Unemployed.

———————————————

It was sixty-five years ago this March that Ira Hayes, USMC, helped raise the American flag on top of Mount Suribachi on Iwo Jima. Hand salute! Ready, two.

———————————————

Our fundraising-storytelling-eating-art-buying event was a success. We wanted to help raise money for Fond du Lac's Ojibwe Language Camp. The learning will be happening at the north end of Big Lake at the newly named Kiwenz Campground. I named it for my grandfather, Mike Shabiash, who we called Kiwenz. Three generations of Jim Northrups mounted the sign identifying the site as Kiwenz Campground. We located it so that if shots are fired at the sign, they will pass through and hit the Chimook houses on the other side of the lake.

My cousin Brenda and her staff had worked hard preparing the center for the evening. Chairs were set up in the gymnasium, and tables and chairs were set up for the silent auction and for eating the feast. Pat Northrup and Ivy Vainio set up the donated art items on the tables and made sure there was a bid sheet and working pens so people could write down what they wanted to spend. Ivy was hovering around the art objects, answering questions. Vickie and Larry Ellis were doing the 50/50 cash raffle. Sarah Agaton Howes and Caleb Dunlap were handling the registration duties. We wanted to create a mailing list so those interested people could hear news of our language camp plans.

Pebaamibines, sometimes known as Dennis Jones started the evening's doings off the right way with a pipe ceremony. Bryon Jon, sometimes known as Bryon Jon, was the other half of the MC team. He used his pipe to also bless our get-together. We gave them a handwritten agenda, and they took it from there. Sandy Shabiash of the RBC was there to welcome the people to the event.

The MC introduced the Northrup Road Players, and we took off with the most recent production of *Shinnob Jep*. We made the audience laugh, we made them cry, and that was all before we even started. The Northrup Road Players had an emergency replacement for the John Johnson Jr. character because our first two choices couldn't act the part. One had to watch TV, and the other wanted to sit on his couch. Randy Gresczyk filled in and acted just good in this production. It seemed like we just got started and it was over.

We had some great storytellers come to Sawyer to tell stories. Among the crowd favorites were Marcie Rendon, Sarah Agaton Howes, Al Hunter, and Frank Montano, also Gordon Jourdain, Rick Gresczyk, Robert Desjarlait,

Mizi-way Desjarlait, Darren Cobenais, Thorne Bordeaux, Wakinyan LaPointe, and Leonard Moose. Among the artists donating their work for the silent auction were Jim Denomie, Steve Premo, Charles Tuna Nahgahnub, Juanita Fineday, Sharon Shabiash, Vickie Ellis, Karen Savage Blue, Gerald White, Pat Northrup, Carrie Estey, Joe Fairbanks, Deb Jones Northrup, Joe Bakademakwa, and Ted Charles.

Arnie Vainio donated a set of wrenches, Rick Gresczyk gave some of his Eagle Works books, and Al Hunter gave a signed book of his works. For the first time since it was built, the Sawyer Center seemed crowded. It was gratifying to see so many people come together without a body lying at the front of the room.

A woman came up to me afterward and told me she was glad she came with her mother. She said since her dad had died the year before, she hadn't seen her mother smile until she heard the storytellers. She added that for the first time in a long time her mother felt proud to be an Anishinaabe.

I know I have written about going to the sugar bush quite a few times over the last few years, but too bad, I am doing it again. I want to let people know about it—the ones who can't go to the sugar bush because of jobs, a judge, or they don't have access to maple trees. It is a big event in my life, so I write about it. I like the way the sugar bush brings the family together. I like the smell of wood smoke; I also like seeing the woods thaw, smell those smells. I like the sound of the wind blowing through the trees, that bird we only hear at sugar bush time. I like hearing the stories told around the fire. Okay, okay, I tell a few stories myself.

We began to prepare for sugar bush last year as we were putting things away from our sugar bush. We recycled our milk jugs we use. We rinsed them in a bleach/water mixture and dried them in the sun. Once they were dry, we put them in large plastic bags and sealed and hung them under the deck . . .

Last fall we buried the cast iron boiling kettle in the ground; about three inches of cast iron kettle was sticking up out of the ground. We tamped the earth around the kettle so it was packed tight. We were making the right-sized fire pit. All we had to do was lift the kettle out from the ground to the right height to boil, had a good pit underneath.

We dried the taps in the sun and put them in the leather pack. I made a few replacements by cutting a maple stick; I brought it home and cut it into the proper lengths. I drilled a hole in the center using my traditional Dewalt 18-volt cordless drill. I then carved the tapered end. I carved a notch to hold the milk jug, and I was done with one tap.

This year my son Joe and nephew Kris were the tapping crew. Kris would drill the holes after he looked at the tree to make sure it wasn't a basswood or oak. Some trees had leaves on them from last fall. Those two would look at that leaf and say Canada. Joe would clean the shavings from the hole and insert a tap that he tap-tapped in with a Buck knife. One of us placed a jug on the tap and we could hear the plunk-plunk sound of falling sap. When I heard that sound, I could smell the wood smoke and taste the syrup already.

We drilled some one day and came back the next and drilled more until we ran out of jugs and taps. Then we settled back and waited for the maple trees to do their part. The crew went to gather the sap. We used five-gallon buckets and barrels to hold our gift. We brought the sap home and unloaded what we had. I like to boil when I have a hundred gallons of sap. Larry and Vickie Ellis came to help with the boiling. I built the fire, and once we had a bed of red coals, we moved the kettle over the fire. We used sticks of firewood around the kettle to keep the heat in the pit. Larry and I added wood or sap as needed. At the end of the day, we had two and a half gallons of syrup. We brought it inside, where my wife Patricia further boiled and filtered our gift. She set some aside to make sugar cakes and canned the little jars that hold the results of our first boil.

The next day we gathered sap and prepared for our next boil. Two of my grandchildren came to help. Miigwech Sarice and Joseph. We had a feast and prepared a manido miijim (spirit dish). We invited friends to come and eat and laugh. Sugar bush is just beginning. Can Corvette season be next? You betcha.

In May, Fond du Lac Follies motored to University of Wisconsin at Superior, our first powwow of the season. Of course, we went through Jay Cooke State Park, with its curvy road. It was also the first top-down ride in that Corvette. But, more about the silver Sting Ray later.

The car took a backseat to the outside we were

feeling and seeing. The just-budding trees were nice to look at, the green of the popple, the red of the birch, and the no-more white of the snow.

We stopped to look at a porcupine. Mr. Gaag was just climbing up then down a maple tree. When he noticed us watching him, he climbed down, always on the other side of the tree from us. He was just doing porcupine stuff. He didn't even bristle his quills at us, was just looking over his shoulder as he walked away.

The Corvette was running just fine. The rumble of the pipes was soothing. Every spring when the Corvette comes out of hibernation, there is always something to fix. This year was an electrical problem. The wrench dude Chad was all over it. With his gauges, shrink-wrapped tape he was able to get all the spark where it was supposed to go. Then it was time to check the oil and transmission fluid and gas up for the first long ride of the season. The Sting Ray went around the corners of the road through Jay Cooke as if it were on rails.

The powwow at UW–Superior was a smaller one. Sometimes those are better for visiting than the big ones. We met people we hadn't seen since 19 and 86. I think the powwow would have been just good if they held it two hundred yards south of the current location, in Weisman Arena. The big difference is between dancing on concrete and dancing on the earth. Another difference is the sounds. The only common theme was the visiting that went on at the powwows, inside or out.

The powwow season begins again. As does the Corvette season.

My wife for life, Patricia, and I motored to Onigamiising (Duluth) for a meal. This wasn't a standard Catholic school dinner; this was a special dinner at Wiigwaasi-Jiiman Wiisiniiwigamig (the Birchbark Canoe Restaurant) in the Tower Building at the College of Saint Scholastica. We were invited by the students of the Ojibwe Language Culture Education program.

We made our reservations from my Reservation. We agreed to meet Dr. Arnie Vainio, wife Ivy, and son Jacob there at 1830 (6:30 PM). We were shown to our table, and our server asked what we would like to drink. I ordered nibi (water) and makademashkikiwaaboo (coffee), my wife had doodooshaaboo (milk) and ziinzibaakwad (sugar) with her coffee.

For our appetitizer, we both had a salad with oil and potato soup, plus bakwezhigan (bread) and doodooshaaboo-bimide (butter). For the main course my wife had lasagna, and I had another bowl of that potato soup. And for dessert we had apple crisp with ice cream, plus I had cake and whipped cream. I waddled out to the car for the trip back to the Reservation. I liked how Bill Howes, his family, and his students put this whole thing together. They served good food and helped preserve Ojibwemowin at the same time.

In April 2010 I turned sixty-seven, ingodwaasimidanaashi-niizhwaaswi nd'biboonigiz. Sometimes those Ojibwemowin words are so long it feels like I will be sixty-eight before I get to the end of the word.

There are two Wisconsin events to write about. The first event happened in Stevens Point, which gives me a chance to ask again who the heck is Stevens and why does he or she get a point. How can I get a point? Pat and I went there to talk about birch bark baskets and attend the powwow.

The second event was a monster. I was invited to recite poetry for the statewide tribute to Vietnam veterans. The event was such a monster they held it in Lambeau Field in Green Bay. The event was called LZ Lambeau. It was an overdue honoring of the veterans' service, dedication, and sacrifices.

We motored to Green Bay in my wife's midsized Buick. It was a bit crowded for us. It was Pat, her sister Cynthia, my son Aaron, and our friend Ivy. She was the official Jim Northrup photographer on this gig.

We found our hotel, set up camp and found Lambeau Field. We saw many bumper stickers. One said All Gave Some, Some Gave All; another said Dysfunctional Veteran: My Medication Protects You. A lot just said Vietnam Veteran.

I walked around there feeling like someone had my back covered. Lambeau Field had 1,244 empty chairs in the middle of the playing field. They represented the Wisconsin people that died in the Vietnam War. I am glad I took pictures of the things I was seeing. The production crew treated us like we were honored guests. They had golf carts to drive us wherever we wanted to go.

On Friday afternoon we rehearsed the program. My voice sounded good with those killer microphones.

Ben E. King sang his "Stand by Me" song. Chris Noel handled the MC duties. I had never met Chris Noel but did know she was a DJ on Armed Forces Vietnam Network. I never heard her, but I am sure the sound of her voice entertained the troops. Kimo Williams sang a Jimmy Hendrix song and stroked his guitar. We rehearsed again on Friday evening. On Saturday we were ushered to the green room; it was stocked with water, coffee, some snacks. We crackered and cheesed. Also groped the grapes.

When it was my turn to talk, I wasn't nervous because I knew I was going to introduce myself in Ojibwemowin. I carried an eagle feather.

I told the assembled veterans why I wrote the poems; I said it was my brain taking a moo.

The first poem was kind of somber. It was about my dead brother who "died in the war but didn't fall down for fifteen tortured years." I then recited "Shrinking Away." That one moved the crowd; I could hear them laughing at the end of each line, had to wait until they finished laughing before I could say the next line. I closed with a poem for the attorney general Richard Blumenthal. That poem is called "Wannabee."

I knew I reached the audience. We connected. I felt so good about that I had to pump my feather in the air a few times as I was walking off stage. My smile could only be removed by a drill instructor.

When everyone was done doing what they do, we all gathered on stage to sing that song by the Animals, "We Gotta Get Out of This Place." I sang along and grooved on the music of the song, the singing. I was on the verge of dancing, even. My wife, Patricia, and

Patty Loew later told me I got a standing ovation. Forty thousand people in a standing O. Wow. I felt honored.

When I went backstage, I began to wait for my golf cart. Governor Doyal, his wife, and his state troopers had first dibs on the golf carts. While I was waiting, I noticed the veterans streaming by on their way out of the stadium. Flash cameras were going off, and I noticed a lot of people looking at me.

I walked toward them, and they began reaching to shake my hand Some told me how powerful my words were. I shook more than a hundred veterans' hands, hugged more than twenty-five women.

On our trip home, we stopped for gas in Wausau, a hundred miles away. A family of four approached and told me how much they enjoyed my words.

My wife told me to turn off my charisma machine so we could get home.

The operation was a success but the patient lived. I went from pre-op to op to post-op rather nicely. The artery doctor came in and initialed my leg so we all knew he would be working on my left leg, which was the right one. I transitioned from pre-op to op, where I was issued an official white party hat to cover my head hair. A gas passer came in and told me what would happen. He would give me gas to sleep and gas to wake me up.

I was wheeled into the op room; lights were hanging from the ceiling, pointed at me, since I was going to be the star in this three-hour show. I saw green-clad nurses hovering around as the black mask descended on my face.

I woke up three hours and thirteen minutes later in the post-op room surrounded by family. They said only stents were needed to open up my leg artery, and I could leave the hospital in the morning.

I told the family members they could go home now because I knew they had put in a long day. I was instructed that I would have to lie flat on the bed to help with the healing of the incision in my right leg artery. It was a four-hour sentence. I felt something and asked if I had a catheter in me. The nurse said yes, but they would remove it in a few hours. I was given ice water to drink. My mouth was really dry. The nurse said it was from the dye that was used to mark the location and size of the blockage and also the gas that put me to sleep and woke me up.

The nurse came back with a good news/bad news story. They said I could get up and walk around after they removed the catheter. I said, okay, remove away. She reached down and quickly pulled the catheter. This caused intense pain that lasted only a few seconds before it went away. I said okay and sat up. She said I could walk around after she unhooked the IV in my left arm.

I felt a little strange after the morphine shot. I felt no pain. The artery has three stainless steel stents in it to keep the passageway open. For me, the worst part of the operation was the removal of the catheter—that and an alleric reaction to the drug Plavix. I got hives and suddenly didn't feel good. All I wanted to do was lie around and mope. The doctors decided on a different drug that would keep my blood flowing without clotting. My wife took me home, where I am recuperating. My leg circulation will improve.

The Second Annual Fond du Lac Reservation language camp was a roaring success. We had at least ten fluent speakers and more than four hundred campers. Patricia did most of the planning, say 95 percent of the work. My part was easy. She would suggest something, and I would say, "That sounds good to me."

We provided three meals a day, and the method we used worked quite well. We asked various families and community centers to provide one meal each. There was more than enough food for the multitudes. Once again, the canoe race was one of the highlights of the camp. I saw one team tip over into the water four times before they got past the dock. It was good the Rez sent game wardens to act as the safety boat, because canoes were tipping over on the way to the turnaround point and back. The Rez museum sent two of the locally made birch bark canoes to the race. Only one of them turned over. We laughed muchly at the racers, especially at Keith Secola, who came all the way from Tempe, Arizona, to tip over. He didn't bring his imaginary brother, Pep. Go ahead, say his brother's whole name out loud.

Indian Country TV sent a crew to film and record the happenings. I am not sure of the technical end of things, but they were able to Livestream a lot of the happenings. Some of the campers were able to learn how to work with the materials in making birch bark baskets. Seven people finished making a small basket. My hooch was next to the flute maker Frank Montano, so I was serenaded all day. Charlie Nahgahnub brought materials for people to make knockers and poles for manoomin. Randy Gresczyk taught about fifteen people how to make hand drums. Carrie Estey showed people how indigenous people made pottery.

We all learned to speak more Ojibwemowin. Bebangii (little by little). Then we began planning for next year's camp.

Aaniin ezhi ayaayan? How are you? Well, alphabetically speaking, I had an abscess in my arse, a boil in my buttocks, a carbuncle in my can, a disaster in my derriere, an eruption in my epidermis, a fissure in my fanny, a gouge in my glutes, a hole in my haunch, and an infection in my interior. I had to have surgical help with my medical malady.

It was the same problem Rathide had. I went to Mino-ayaawin clinic and talked to the doctor. He took notes and asked if the wound was draining. I thought it was, and he prescribed an antibiotic after the examination. He suggested a hot bath to ease the pain. Apparently the wound closed up and continued to fester inside. The doctor said I should get to the emergency room right away.

My wife took me to the emergency room in Cloquet hospital, and the doctor there said she thought I should be examined by a surgeon. They called an ambulance, and I was transported to Saint Mary's in Duluth. What? An ambulance for my burning bum, my painful posterior? Fortunately they didn't use the red lights and siren. That was the first time I ever rode to Duluth wearing just a medical gown.

I was examined by two doctors, one of whom was a surgeon. I was wheeled into surgery right away. They issued me a white party hat for my head hair. Once again I met the gas passer, who put me to sleep. I woke up after about ninety minutes. The surgeon explained that my wound was rather deep and I would need to be packed with medicated gauze so the wound would heal from the bottom out.

The next morning I was released, and the pain pills were doing what they were supposed to do. No pain nowhere. Nurses from three different agencies examined and attended to my wound. The hole healed from the bottom of my bottom out, as it was supposed to. Like Rathide, no more dual exhausts.

Fond du Lac Follies motored to Saint Paul to attend the Native American Journalists Association convention. The doings were held in the Crown Royal Hotel. I began seeing Indians as soon as I walked into the lobby, so I knew I was in the right place. I called Ray Earley to join me; I knew we would get good eats there. We did.

I was invited to be the plenary speaker. Didn't know what that was so I looked it up in the dictionary. I told stories for an hour. One friend I met there was Dan Agent, a former editor of his tribe's newspaper. About fifteen years ago, he was fired because of something he ran in the newspaper. I wrote about freedom of the press in Indian Country at the time. Since then, a new administration came in and did include that freedom. They are now celebrating ten years of freedom of the press in Cherokee country.

Here at Fond du Lac, we don't have freedom of the press. Right on the masthead of our Rez newspaper we are told no letters to the editor are allowed, no opinion pieces, either.

We have a ways to go before we have freedom of the press here.

This summer I wanted to check the manoomin in one of my secret spots. I chose to show my nephew that spot so he could claim it as his secret spot when I am gone. Kris was raised in the city; he finally returned home a few years back. Now the family has to Indianize him, teach him what he should have learned when he was younger.

We launched the canoe on a river that was east-southwestnorth of the Rez. I showed Kris a few things about paddling. When I heard the clunk of the paddle hitting the canoe, I reminded him we don't do that.

The river had a clear channel down the middle and manoomin beds along each bank. The beds went on for more than a mile. The river smelled just rivery. The blue sky was broken up by white puffy clouds traveling east with the wind.

We paddled downstream with the current. The turtles on the rocks and deadhead logs slid in the water as we approached. A blue heron flew down the river with majestic sweeps of his wings. The manoomin invited us over for a closer look. The plants were growing real close together. For our return to the landing, we didn't paddle much. We let the wind blow us home. I dipped a paddle occasionally to steer and to keep us from getting sideways in the wind. So in that lazy afternoon canoe ride, Kris learned about manoomin and paddling a canoe. Now he will have something to teach his son Makoons.

━━━━━━━━━━━━━━━━━━━━━━━━━

The little village of Sawyer is changing right before our eyes. Remember that old gravel pit that was dug in the 1940s to construct Mission Road? Well, now it is a new gravel pit. The gravel is being used to reconstruct Moorhead Road in Sawyer.

━━━━━━━━━━━━━━━━━━━━━━━━━

With other Sawyer community members, Fond du Lac Follies bussed to Minneapolis. We went to watch a football game. The Minnesota Vikings were going to play the Miami Dolphins.

When we went down with the community before to a football game, we had a luxury coach. The kind of coach that has a bathroom in the back. This time we were in a shorter bus, and it wasn't long before people were talking about being in the short bus.

I was feeling a bit of culture shock being there mixed into the crowd of 63,815 people. Actually I only counted 63,750. On the way in, I got a tub of popcorn for the amazing price of seven bucks. I noticed beer was selling for seven bucks a bottle. It would be difficult to be a drunk there, I thought.

We weren't in the nosebleed section, but we could smell it. This wasn't the most spectacular game I ever saw, wasn't even in the top hundred. The Vikings played but didn't win. The less said, the better.

Coming from a large extended family means I go to a lot of funerals. There were two deaths in our community in the last month.

My cousin Sylvia stopped by for a visit. She is almost seventy years old. Sylvia has known me all of my life. How are we cousins, you might ask? Well, her dad was my grandma's brother. We had coffee at the kitchen table, the morning sunshine came through the windows as we talked and laughed. There was a smell of bacon grease in the air because Pat was cooking breakfast. We talked about our mutual experiences as runaways from federal boarding schools.

She attended Flandreau when she was a little girl. So, Sylvia and her chums decided to run away from the school. It was a very dark night when they began walking across the prairie. Sylvia was leading, and she said it was too dark to see her hands, so they walked real slow. It was quiet in the night until Sylvia walked into a cow. The quiet ended because the cow bellowed and Sylvia screamed. Her chums screamed when they heard her scream. The girls turned around and ran back toward the boarding school. We both laughed when she ended her story.

Cousin Leo Peterson has always been my hero because of his quiet nature and bravery. He was about seven years older than me. How are we cousins, you might ask? Well, his dad and my other grandma were brother and sister. I knew he had served in the US Army as a paratrooper. He continued the family tradition of serving in the military. Because of his example, I joined the US Marines as soon as I turned eighteen. I didn't want to jump out of an airplane, I wanted to jump into the Marines.

I was always told by my grandparents how I was related to different people in the community. I find myself doing that now with my children and grandchildren.

We celebrated the Marine Corps's birthday. The Fond du Lac–area Marines, gyrenes, leathernecks, seagoing bell-hops, jarheads, grunts, and Ogichidaag of the area felt the thrill of saying Gung ho to one another. We had a Marine Corps ball celebrating 235 years of Marine Corps history. The event was held at the Fond du Lac Reservation Golf Course Clubhouse. I don't know of any other Rez besides the Navajo that does this. I think the bulk of the credit should be directed at my cousin Trapper; he was in Iraq as a combat Marine. I am sure the Rez veterans service officer helped organize the celebration.

We begin eating to begin the celebration. I started seeing Marines I hadn't seen in years. Various thoughts and phrases began firing through my brain housing group randomly:

Improvise, adapt, overcome, Eat the apple—you know the rest, Secure your gear, The smoking lamp is lit for one cigarette and I am going to have that one, L-shaped ambush, Front toward enemy, If the army or the navy ever look on heaven's scenes, they will find their wives are sleeping with the United States Marines, Ditty Bopper, Hooch, Rubber Lady, Mighty Mite, 106, Tank, Otter, Amtrac, Brasso, Renew, Peter Boat, APA, Wet net, Mike Boat, Ontos, Gungy, skating, H and S,

Hide and slide, Splib dude, Chucks, Chief, Pepper Gut, Pineapple, Pogey Bait, Slop Chute, Brig Rat, Sea Lawyer, Humping one more click, Smokey the bear hat, Bad Time, In the rear with the beer, BCD, Gunny, Danang, An Hoa, Honcho, Frozen Chosen, Hue City, Tet, Short timer, Little Agony, Big Agony, Mid-rats, Letter Company, Six By, Jodi, Boom-boom, Purple Hurt, Idiot Award, 8th and I, Butter Bar, Railroad Tracks, Rockers, K-Bar, Sandbagging, Skivy shirts, Boonies, Boondockers, Rough Side Out, Semper Fi, Always Faithful, Semper Gumby, Always Flexible, PRC-6, PRC-10, Chow hound, Mess Duty, snuffy, Field Day, Junk on the Bunk, By your leave, sir, Things on the springs, Stacks on the Racks, John Wayne Cs, Canteens, 782 Gear, Grunt, Short rounds, Maggies drawers, Hashmarks, The Suck, Cattle Cars, Office Hours, UCMJ, Special Courts, Field jacket, CS Gas, Brown Side out, Green side out, As you were, Battle Dressing, Recon by fire, MPCs and Ps, O dark 30, Miltary crest, Fighting hole, Fix bayonets, Liberty Call, I'll grab you by your stacking swivel and shake up your nomenclature, Give me a hus, You're bouncing ladies, Heels, heels, heels, Vertical butt stroke, MCRD, Hold 'em and squeeze 'em, First Shirt, Ambush, patrols, Sneak and peek, Better you than me, Body Count.

The final course was the Marine Corps cake. A Marine who served in Vietnam read the message from the commandant. The oldest Marine present and the youngest cut the cake using an NCO sword. We were following the traditions we had learned over the years. The oldest Marine was from World War II, the youngest was from the Iraq/Afghanistan wars.

The bar was open all evening, and I didn't see anyone overdo it. We sang the "Marines' Hymn," I got misty-eyed. I think we all walked out of there at the end of the evening with our backs a little straighter, our shoulders a little back, our paces a thirty-inch step. Our eyes were a little narrower, as if we were looking for enemies. Two hundred thirty-five years old? Heck, Marine, you don't look a day over two hundred.

Chapter 10

Tickled a Little Moo
Out of Me—2011

Fond du Lac Follies jetted to Tennessee on my last airline ride. It was the latest fed scare and choice, called back-scatter X-ray or enhanced pat-downs. Strange, just about the time the feds are done using the colored security placards warning of terrorist (bogeyman) insurgents attacks.

When I first checked on an airline ticket, I was quoted a price for the trip, there and back. By the time I purchased the tickets, the cost had risen a bit more than two hundred bucks in two weeks.

At the Minneapolis airport, I found a long walk to the gate. I entered the queue for the first metal screening, hoping the stainless steel stents in an artery wouldn't set off the alarm. I removed the metal from my pockets, took off my shoes, and walked through the machine. I walked through okay, but my carry-on bag had to go through twice and a hand search was required. I got dressed while the blueshirts passed my bag along.

Then I had an airport choice: radiation or fondling. Guilty until proven innocent? I was looking forward to saying at the end of the TSA fondling, Okay, my turn now. While waiting to be fondled, I noticed a third choice. Passengers were choosing a third line between the other two choices. I joined the opt-out line. We just walked between both of them and went to our gates to wait to get on the airplanes.

In Bristol, Tennessee, I met Tonya Stansberry and her daughter Hannah. They were southern hospitality personified. They made me feel welcome by taking me to Bristol Motor Speedway for a tour. I got to ride around the track in the pace car, a blue-and-white Mustang. I asked my host if I could drive; him said no. My host drove us around and his tires began to slip on the rain-soaked track. Uh-oh. That part almost tickled a little moo out of me. We parked by the 33-degree-angle banked track. I climbed up to the top of the race track. I looked around, then carefully, using baby steps, walked back down. I was worried about taking a tumble down to the pace car. We toured the owner's skybox and oohed and aahed over that place. It looked like about a hundred NASCAR fans could have watched the races from there. We then went for a ride down the quarter mile of the Thunder Valley drag strip. It was a fun tour. Of course, I was wondering what my Corvette would have done there. I went back to the motel and slept fast because the next day looked like it was going to be a busy one.

I did a reading in an auditorium, then an interview in a TV studio, a quick lunch, then I visited an English composition class. There was a feast prepared by the members of the English Department. The meal was topped off with a huge orange cake that had Welcome, Jim Northrup lettered on the top. I then did an evening campuswide reading and answered a few questions from the audience. Once again, I slept fast because I could go home in the morning. At the airport I didn't have to make a choice between backscatter radiation or fondling. I went through the normal screening and got on the airplane. I changed planes in Chicago and was back in Sawyer by noon. It was a quick visit to Tennessee, but I made some new friends who will be coming up for our Ojibwe language camp.

I guess it ain't bragging if you done it, but I heard from a very good source that the video *LZ Lambeau*, which documented Wisconsin's salute to Vietnam veterans, won an Emmy. I am proud to say I had a small part in the production. I spoke in Ojibwemowin to introduce myself and then recited three poems. Congrats to Patty Loew of Wisconsin Public Television and the rest of the crew that made *LZ Lambeau*.

In a related video note, I also learned that the movie shot at the Fond du Lac Reservation called *Older Than America* is now available for purchase from Amazon and a few other places. I liked Georgina's movie because they had my wife and son, my house, my fire pit, and my Corvette and friends in that movie. I heard myself reciting my one line. I rehearsed that line for weeks, and I think I nailed it: "Why, you got a crime to report or are the cops looking for you, too?" It was good to see Wes Studi, Adam Beach, Georgina Lightning, Tantoo Cardinal, and Ray Earley on the big screen again.

I was shocked by the event in Tucson, Arizona, where six people were killed and eighteen were wounded by a deranged gunman. I wasn't shocked by the fact that it happened, because events like these are becoming quite common in America. What shocked me was the nonstop coverage of the shootings and the aftermath. The media feeding frenzy went on for longer than two weeks.

What shocked me was the fact that Americans were also being wounded and killed in Afghanistan, and not one word was mentioned in the mainstream media about them.

As a Marine, I was wondering how many of my fellow Marines had died in the past month in that undeclared war. I could not find the numbers anywhere. Does this mean the deaths only count when they happen in a shopping mall? I sure hope not.

Why don't we know about the deaths from overseas? Is it some kind of state secret? Are the families of the servicemen the only ones impacted?

If we begin to question the number of Americans killed, shouldn't we also ask the question, why? Why did they die in Afghanistan?

There was a double homicide in Cromwell, a village about ten miles west of Sawyer. In writing about the terrible crime, the *Duluth News Tribune* stated the shooting happened near the boundary of the Fond du Lac Indian Reservation. I read it again and couldn't see why that bit of information was included in the story. Was the newspaper trying to stir up some racial hatred?

The killer or killers are unknown at this time so there was no reason to include the Reservation or Fond du Lac people in the story.

I wrote an e-mail to a reporter from the newspaper; she kicked my e-mail upstairs to her boss. In the e-mail, I asked if they used editors down there anymore. A couple days later, I got an e-mail from Robin Washington, editor of the Duluth newspaper. He agreed that the reference to the Fond du Lac Indian Reservation shouldn't have been in the story.

He further explained that one of his reporters talked with our chair, Karen Diver. The reporter asked her if the Fond du Lac Police were helping with the investigation. That was supposed to be part of the story, but somehow it wasn't. So, the reference to the Fond du Lac Indian Reservation wasn't germane to the story.

Robin Washington said the reference to the Fond du Lac Indian Reservation was removed from the online version of the newspaper. He said it was a teachable moment.

He told me I was right.

While driving home from the Sawyer Community Center I pulled off the road to watch a bald eagle make circles in the sky. I watched that magnificent bird for a couple of minutes, his white head and tail, black body, stood out from the blue sky above him. He was just coasting along with the wind, doing eagle stuff.

I drove home, quietly thrilled by the encounter. Migizi.

We gathered again for winter storytelling. Rick

Gresczyk brought a pink piece of paper and handed it out because it was so close to Valentine's Day. It was titled "Ojibwe for Lovers" and contains such phrases as:

- *Nanda-noojikaazodaa.* Let's go snagging.
- *Aapiji gimiikawaadiz.* You are so beautiful.
- *Geget, ninibwaakaa gaye.* Yes, that's right. I'm smart, too.
- *Giminwenim ina?* Do you like me?
- *Bangii eta go giminwenimin.* I only like you a little.
- *Bi-wiijiiwishin.* Come, be with me.
- *Geyaabi na gizaagi'?* Do you still love me?
- *Eya', aapiji gizaagi'in.* Yes, I really love you.
- *Ninoondendam.* I am in a flirtatious mood.
- *Giin dash?* How about you?
- *Minjimishin niinimoshenh.* Hold me, my sweetheart.
- *Daga giziiyaabide'on.* Why don't you brush your teeth?
- *Giwii-ojiim ina?* Do you want to kiss me?
- *Giwii-ojiimin.* I want to kiss you.
- *Ojiimishin gagiibaadiz.* Kiss me, you fool.
- *Giga-mino-bimaadizimin.* We shall have a good life.

I first heard about the proposed PolyMet open pit mine some years ago, and just as I feared, it is getting closer and closer to becoming a reality. I hear they plan to use a sulfide mixture to leach out the precious metals they find once they start crushing rocks. As I understand it, the process will require a lot of water. Hundreds of thousands of gallons of water a day, by one estimate. And where does the water/sulfide mixture go once they are done leaching? It goes into huge holding ponds. The holding ponds, like anything else made by man, can break and leak. Where does the water/sulfide mixture go then? Into the bogs, creeks, and rivers that are downhill from the holding ponds.

One of the rivers near the site is the the Saint Louis River, which defines our northern and eastern boundaries on this Reservation. Where does the water/sulfide mixture go after that? Into the fish, the deer, the plants and animals that drink from that river. The water could then enter my personal food chain because I eat fish, deer meat, and wild rice and other plants.

With that in mind, I decided to attend the mining forum held at the Fond du Lac Tribal and Community College. The forum participants were from PolyMet, the Great Lakes Indian Fish and Wildlife Commission (GLIFWC), and the Fond du Lac Reservation. I went because I wanted to know who would be trying to poison me with a water/sulfide mixture. I wanted to hear what the people from PolyMet would say. A representative from GLIFWC started by explaining how mining works and showed pictures and maps from various other mines in the 1837/1854 ceded territories. Here on the Rez, we are downstream from PolyMet. We learned more about mining from Fond du Lac's environmentalist Nancy Sthuldt. We also learned how Fond du Lac would be involved in making sure the mining operation was done without poisoning me.

Brad Moore, from PolyMet, was next up and he told the PolyMet story. Finally, chair Karen Diver spoke about how PolyMet would have to meet all environmental regulations and what Fond du Lac would do to protect us and our resources. Her talk was stopped by bursts of applause from the crowd. The evening ended with questions from the audience. Everyone was invited to the front of the room to say what they were thinking. As for me, after listening all evening to all sides at the forum, I came to the conclusion that I never met a PolyMet I liked.

Finally it was time to tap maple trees. I have been watching for the right time, and sugar bush is finally here. The thermometer registered the right temps; the trees had a melted circle around the base of the trees. The only thing missing was the noisy crows in the morning. I tapped two test trees in my yard to help me watch for sugar bush. After a couple days of checking, Pat noticed the sap was dripping. Belatedly I began hearing the crows. We got to get together and circumcise our watches so we all start at the same time.

I rounded up my sugar bush crew and we went to the woods. The crew knew what to do, and we tapped some trees.

This time we made a startling discovery. Oscar was running in the snow, and the snow was cutting his tender little wiener-dog feet. We were also afraid he might sneak off into the woods and join the local wolf pack as the new alpha male. He is grounded from the sugar bush until the snow melts. The dripping from the taps will continue until then, usually.

Question: Is your bush dripping?
Answer: Never mind, you dirty old man.

I usually write my column once a month, but occasionally I don't. I took the month off to celebrate my sixty-eighth birthday. So Sioux me.

Graduation season is upon us, and I just have to brag. My son Matthew Northrup graduated from Fond du Lac Tribal and Community College and was one of the commencement speakers. He won a slug of awards for his 4.0 grade point average. He wants to keep going to school until he has a *Dr.* in front of his name. I am sure proud of him. James W. Northrup IV will graduate from Cloquet High School next week. Niiwin, as we call him, also makes me proud.

The Mother Earth Water Walkers came walking along the northern border of the Fond du Lac Reservation. This group was carrying a copper bucket of nibi (water) from the Pacific Ocean. They were going to join with walkers who were carrying water from the Atlantic Ocean, the Carribean, and the Pacific Ocean. Walkers from different points of the compass were going to meet at the Bad River Reservation in northern Wisconsin.

While driving to meet them on Highway 2, I

thought of the water I used to carry. I was young, maybe eleven years old, when I was introduced to carrying nibi. The house we lived in did not have running water. That was when, as the oldest boy in the family, I learned it was my duty to go after nibi. We had electricity but no running water. There were ten kids running around but we had no running water. Year after year, I supplied the water for my family. I carried so much nibi I thought my name was Nadoobii.

The nearest water was at my gramma's brother's house. My great-uncle had a well and a pump. Jim Blacketter said we could use his pump and get all the nibi we needed.

I would use two cream cans, both about thirty-five gallons in size. I would use the hand pump to fill a bucket and pour it into the cream cans. I continued pumping and pouring until the cream cans were full. In the spring, summer, and fall I would use a wagon to transport the nibi. In the winter I used either a sled or toboggan.

I really disliked clothes washing and bath days; with that many kids in the house it was always someone's turn to take a bath. I didn't feel sorry for myself—it wouldn't have done any good—so I just carried water.

I found the Shinnobs carrying nibi just west of Floodwood. I saw a man carrying an eagle staff and a woman carrying a small bucket of water. They were walking along the shoulder of the road with a pickup in front and one behind. I joined the group and idled along behind the last truck. I recognized some of the people in the group. I saw my indoozhimis, my sister Doris's daughter. We call her Debbie Do. I also saw Lynn Olson from Fond du Lac. Esther Humprey from

Leech Lake was also part of the nibi carriers. The women looked proud when it was their turn to carry the water.

I think the nibi walkers accomplished their mission of making people aware of how important water is. As they said, nibi is sacred.

As I mentioned, it is time to make baskets. My sons have been very helpful in gathering the raw materials for nooshkachinaaganike.

One day, sons Matthew and Aaron and I went to our secret location for good bark. It was a little early in the season, and each tree had to be coaxed to give up the bark. We made an offering of tobacco before we started gathering. I was able to show my sons how patience and a sharp knife are used to slowly remove the bark. We gathered about fifteen good sheets of bark.

I brought the bark home, and Pat and I examined it closely. I laid out and formed the baskets and she sewed the corners up. I then attached the willow sticks and used them as a guide to cut away the parts that didn't look like a basket. Pat then sewed the characteristic V-stitch around the top rim to finish the basket. They sure look good hanging on my wall, but they won't stay there long; someone always buys whatever we make. I wonder where this year's baskets will end up.

The Third Annual Nagaajiwanaang Ambe Anishi-naabemodaa language camp at Kiwenz Campground in

Sawyer was just good. More than five hundred people showed up to teach or learn Ojibwemowin. Some came for the art and learned moccasin making, ricing tool making, quillworking, birch bark basket making, and how to make a drumstick.

One young boy, about eight years old, came by to show me his drumstick. He brought along the hand drum he had made at last year's language camp. Randy Gresczyk was the teacher for both. He was proud as he was tapping out a beat on his drum with his new drumstick.

News from Indian Country TV has videos of the canoe race, the personal favorite of mine. This year, my son Jim came in first with the rice pole race and second in the paddle race. He and his canoe partner, Willard Fools Bull, split 180 bucks for their efforts. Willard is a Lakota from Pine Ridge Reservation, and this was his first time in a canoe.

NFIC TV also has a video of the nature walk and many other activities from the camp. On our last day of the camp, Sunday, Gary Farmer stopped by for a visit. He and his band, the Troublemakers, were headed for White Earth after his appearance at Fond du Lac. He spoke to the assembled campers and told us we were doing the right thing because preservation was so important.

The annual Fond du Lac veterans powwow was a smooth summertime event. Once again it was held in Sawyer on the shores of Big Lake—Gichi-zaaga' igan, Doc Rick likes to call it. My wife didn't put up her food stand called Stand Here. Instead she danced for all the veterans in her family.

My son Aaron sold soda pop and water to the people who came to the powwow. It was a good move on his part because the hot weather made his stand a popular place.

I was right next door to him in my veterans' lounge. The sign saying Free Coffee for Veterans was up, and we had a lot of people stopping by for that. We had shade and chairs in the lounge, and different veterans visited and told stories about their time in the military.

Two close friends spent a lot of time there, Ray Earley and Ted Charles. We were Marines during the Vietnam War. Ray is from White Earth and Ted is from Gallup, New Mexico. The veterans' lounge floor was littered with empty C-ration cans, grenade pins, and brass by the time we were done telling stories.

It is a beautiful summer morning, and I am listening to Robert Johnson and his blues guitar. I am writing the Follies while jamming along. The sun is shining on my left arm, the dogs, Oscar and his dog, Belle, are barking at whatever dogs bark at. I am drinking coffee and wondering what I shall write about this time, so let's go, see what comes out while under the influence of blues and caffeine.

This year we have had some visitors who were slightly out of the ordinary.

First, of course, was Gary Farmer. He wanted a weekend away from his teaching duties in Sioux

Lookout, Canada. He wanted to relax and perhaps play a little poker at the Black Bear Casino.

For those who don't know Gary, think movies and *Pow Wow Highway* or *Smoke Signals*. Gary Farmer ate, slept, talked, and charmed everyone he met in Sawyer, including my sister-in-law Cynthia Dow, who was visiting from Morton, Minnesota. Cynthia visits all the time, so she is an ordinary visitor. Gary liked the Black Bear Casino, where he won enough at poker to pay for the gasoline he burnt to get here and back.

Charlie Hill and his brother Rick were the next surprise visitors. Charlie came to Sawyer to meet some Navajos who were visiting my son Jim. As long as he was in the area, Charlie decided to drop in to the World Headquarters of the Fond du Lac Follies. Charlie has been making people laugh since the late '70s, and our trails have crossed quite a few times since then. Of course, both of those guys had to have a ride in the '64 Corvette. I took Charlie to the S-turn road south of Sawyer. He didn't scream as we went around the corners, but I know he wanted to. We ate together, and the two Hill brothers motored back to Wisconsin.

The visitor who traveled the farthest to visit the World Headquarters was Mary Modeen, a well-known artist and college teacher. Mary teaches at the University of Dundee, Scotland. She lives in Blairgowrie. Mary and I sat at the kitchen table, and I learned her mother was a Jackson and her grandmother was a Grasshopper, and both of them were from Fond du Lac. I told her I was related to some Jacksons and we might be some kind of cousins.

I was stitching on a basket, so it wasn't long before I gave her an awl, some basswood sewing strips, and some birch bark. She learned how to sew birch bark with basswood bark.

After the sewing lesson, Mary and I took a Corvette ride. We went to Kiwenz Campground, and I showed her where we had our language camp. I invited her to come to the next one, in June 2012. She took one of our fanning baskets with her back to Scotland. It was named Gichimiskwaakozi (Big Red). When she left, my wife asked if it was celebrity week on Northrup Road. I smiled.

Fond du Lac Follies motored to Oklahoma with my family. I had been invited to Tahlequah by Richard Allen, a Marine who had served during the Vietnam War. He asked if I could talk about that war and recite some of my poetry. I said shore.

So, we took a road trip. We estimated the distance as 850 miles, mostly interstate. Our plan was each driver would do 200 miles then trade off. That worked well for us, and we got to see Minnesota, Iowa, and Missouri from the four-lane highway. We only stopped for fuel for the car and us.

Near Joplin, we continued following our planned highway to meet a highway that led to Tahlequah. We didn't know two states had the same highway number, and we found ourselves in Arkansas. The road narrowed and at times rock ledges covered both lanes of the highway. They were huge chunks of rocks that had fallen off the ledges in both ditches. On that dark, narrow highway I thought I heard banjo music from the movie

Deliverance. We were glad when we found the highway that went to Tahlequah.

It was hot there, and the sun was merciless. The temps were in excess of a hundred degrees, and we noticed the people didn't walk, they sauntered. So right away we tried to saunter. After a while we got good at sauntering. We leisurely strolled along. One of the places we strolled to was one of the Cherokee's casinos. We won enough at the slots to buy a tank of gasoline.

One of the places we sauntered to was the Cherokee Cultural Center. There we learned more about the history of the Cherokee people. We also met Richard Allen and shared a roast pork feast and listened to some Cherokee singers.

The following morning, we motored to the university, where the day's events were being held. I did my part by speaking and handing out manoomin.

The next day we went home.

Manoominike mii omaa, we are making rice right here in Sawyer. The lakes were bountiful, and there were many pleased ricers. The Rez was buying rice at four bucks a pound.

On one day, when I crawled out of my sickbed, the average canoe came in with fifty-five pounds of rice. Patricia, the old pro, came in with eighty-four pounds. She was ricing with my son Jimmy. He is the guy who won the rice pole race at the language camp last June. We will eat good manoomin until next ricing.

We set up our rice camp in the yard, where we always

set it up. My son Aaron and nephew Kris put the kettle just the way I like it. I didn't have to tell them how to do anything, but I was ready to. It wasn't long before the smell of wood smoke and parching rice was wafting through the yard. We parched and parched. Channel 10 from Duluth came out to film what we were doing, I made it a point to park the Corvette so it would be part of the show.

Aaron and Kris rebuilt the dancing pit, and the dancing and fanning commenced. We had a lot of people who came to learn how we make rice. There were even some students from Germany who came to spend some time in the dancing pit. They didn't come just to learn how to make rice; we were just part of their exchange program from Cloquet High School.

I am glad we make rice like this every year. Wouldn't dream of selling our rice to the Rez, even if they were offering eight bucks a pound.

When President Obama predicted the end of the Iraq war I asked, Did we win? Did we lose? Or did we just lose interest in a war that just kept ambling on and on, one that cost billions of dollars and lives?

Was it worth it? Did we ever find those pesky weapons of mass destruction? How many Americans died in that long-lasting war? I know who suffered besides the Iraqis—it was the combat veterans who came home greatly affected by their experiences.

According to the news, more than 4,000 Americans died and more than 150,000 Iraqi citizens. The cost of the war was estimated at $400 billion.

But alas, the war was not over. Now I hear America is sending troops into Africa, four different countries. And what about Afghanistan—aren't Americans still getting wounded and dying there? I forget why we were even there in the first place.

Do we always have to be at war somewhere?

Awesome. As a word guy, I have watched that word become meaningless. Today I think it has become the equivalent to the phrase *Uh-huh*, what someone says while listening to a long, boring story.

For example . . . I cut my toenails today . . . awesome . . . or, I cleaned my belly button lint . . . oooh, super awesome.

That word *awesome* even flashes on the screen when one wins more than a certain amount on a slot machine at my casino.

Since it is boring to whine without a solution, I hereby propose one. Instead of automatically saying *awesome* when someone quits talking, say *Maamakaaj*, a perfectly good Ojibwe word my dictionary defines as "astonishing." Try it. It is easy to say, and it carries more meaning than that silly old *awesome*. Maamakaaj.

My Rez has a radio station, 89.1 on everyone's FM dial; WGZS are the call lettters. I haven't seen the actual physical layout, although I hear it is at Fond du Lac Ojibwe school. One day soon I will make a visit to the studio.

The voice I hear mostly belongs to Pam Belgarde. I know she is from Turtle Mountain, North Dakota. I met her back in the '90s, when she was working with Deb Wallwork, who was shooting a video called *Warriors: Native American Vietnam Vets.* It was shot for Prairie Public Television of Fargo, North Dakota. Pam was the narrator for that video.

Pam has been coming to our Thursday night language table and is learning Ojibwe words to use on the radio. This will be a learning tool for all of us who listen to the radio.

So far, I have heard her introduce herself in Ojibwemowin, and hearing our language was like music to my ears—no wait, the music was music to my ears. So far the music has been classic rock and powwow songs. The language I heard made me proud to be an Anishinaabe.

As for future plans, I hear they will expand the hours and feature other programs like *Native America Calling.* And also I hear we will be able to hear WGZS on our computers.

This year, the Marine Corps Birthday Ball was celebrated on Northrup Road by two Marines, Ray Earley and myself. On November 10, 2011, we gathered to celebrate with other Marines around the world. We sat at the kitchen table and told each other war stories from the Vietnam War. At 1800, the oldest and youngest Marines present came forward to cut the birthday cake. Since it was just Ray and I, it was easy to figure out who were the oldest and youngest Marines present.

Following Marine Corps tradition, we used an NCO sword to cut the cake. The cake itself was decorated in the campaign ribbon colors of the Vietnam War.

That day, Keith Secola invited me to Fitgers bar in Duluth to be the spoken-word portion of his appearance there. He told me we would take the stage right after the dancers. Belly dancers in Duluth? After playing three songs, Keith invited me up to the stage to recite some poetry. I introduced myself in Ojibwemowin and recited four poems to much applause. That has got to be one of the weirdest places I ever recited my poetry.

One thing about the holiday season that really jerked my chain (to borrow a cliché) was the elder's Christmas party, held at the convention center of the Black Bear Casino—not all of it, but just one part. We usually avoid all things Christmas in this family because we don't celebrate that holiday. We do celebrate people passing out money and a free meal, however, so we went to the Black Bear Casino.

We motored to the Bear and signed up for the goodies. I was given an envelope that contained twenty-five bucks in greenbacks, a coupon good for ten more, and a ticket for the drawing for baskets full of goods prepared by the Reservation employees.

A free meal was also part of the deal, so we set up camp at a round table near the food. Family members drifted in and joined us at our table. I had a son Jim, a grandson Niiwin, and his intended, Aurora, a brother Russ and his wife Deb, one sister Susan and her husband,

Ringo, from Red Lake, a cousin, Butch Martineau, and a visitor named Lester Black Horse, a Dine from Utah. I was able to ignore the Christmas music that permeated the convention center. I frowned at family members I caught singing along with the pervasive music. Hum Bahbug, yes, I am the Grinch who stole Christmas and hid it somewhere.

Before we ate, we listened to someone pray for the feast. I was wondering who was going to pray. Then I heard Sister Rose was going to bless the food. Wait a minute. I heard the Reservation Business Committee had passed a resolution naming Ojibwemowin the official language of the Reservation. If so, why did we borrow a Catholic to pray in English for us? That is what jerked my chain about the elder's party.

Two RBC members were working the crowd. When they came by our round table, I expressed my displeasure at hearing a prayer in English when we could have heard a prayer in Ojibwe. With more than seven hundred people there, we couldn't find one person to pray in our language? Are we so far gone we don't need white people to assimilate us anymore, we do it ourselves? Jeez, I hope not.

Question: What is the difference between a Ponsford wedding and a Ponsford funeral?
Answer: One less mouth to feed.
(Submitted by Ray J. Earley, White Earth Ojibwe who should get all of the praise or blame.)

We stumbled across a pot of money, Jack. We could do nothing better with it than winterize our grandchildren. From the top of their heads to the bottoms of their feet, we bought them some warm. Now we feel warm inside because we were able to do this.

As predicted, the war in Iraq is over. President Obama lived up to his word. I am still stuck in the looking-for-weapons-of-mass-destruction mode. I guess we didn't find them, but they aren't important anymore. Only time will tell if this war of choice was worth it. Meanwhile, the veterans of this war will carry their memories to the grave.

As a Marine veteran of the Vietnam War, I watched the news where four Marines in Afghanistan were pictured urinating on three bodies. War is terrible, and terrible things happen. I think the Marines were aiming at the wrong targets. They should have been aiming at the politicians who put them in harm's way, perhaps the war profiteers who are raking in millions of dollars.

Can anyone tell me why our young men and women are in Afghanistan? What is the purpose of this war of choice? How will we know if we have won or lost?

Instead of carrying a camera to the firefight, I think the Marines should have carried more ammo.

Question: What do you call a Shinnob without a woman?
Answer: Homeless.

Carl Gawboy has written a play called *The Great Hurt*. It is about boarding schools. I have long admired his work as a painter, even used one of his paintings on the front cover of *Walking the Rez Road* when it was reprinted. This play was showing a new facet of his talents. I made plans to attend a reading of his play in Duluth, at the College of Saint Scholastica, Mitchell Auditorium, because I was a boarding school survivor.

Then, in a late afternoon surprise, I got a phone call from Carl himself. He asked if I would read what I had written about my boarding school experiences. I said shore (which in a Minnesota accent means "sure").

Carl said he would send me a script and asked if I would dress all in black. I looked at my wardrobe and decided that would be easy to do because I have a lot of black clothes. That might be a survival mechanism because of our long Minnesota winters, or I could still be honoring Johnny Cash's memory.

On the night of the event, I took only a small part of my extended family to the doings. I took one wife, two sons, one daughter-in-law, and one nephew. We got there in time to miss rehearsal, but since I was reading my words I knew, it would be real easy. The doings started of with a welcome song by the Little Horse Singers.

After some introductory remarks, the readers began reading the words of Captain Pratt of Carlisle and some students from that school and time period.

I read my words. My part was about Pipestone federal boarding school near the town of Pipestone, Minnesota. After the other readers painted the grim picture of boarding schools, I told a story about running away and my recapture. Later, as an adult, I learned area residents were paid a bounty for recapturing runaways. Before I recited my poem "Ditched," I asked the boarding school survivors in the audience to stand for a moment.

There was a discussion about boarding school, with questions from the audience.

There was a reception following the traveling song by the Little Horse Singers. I felt glad to share my sad history of boarding schools.

Fond du Lac Follies motored to Green Bay, Wisconsin, to take part in some veterans' doings. Dan King, the Oneida veterans service officer, had asked me to come and talk about my time in the military and to recite some poetry. Dan and I had walked on the same veterans' trails in years past. Patricia traveled with me.

It was easy to get to Green Bay because we traveled in between the snowstorms. We googled our way across Wisconsin and checked into the casino hotel when we arrived.

We were driven to the Supper Club, where the doings were held. The reception we received from the Oneida veterans was mamaakaaj, truly astonishing. We were treated like rock-star royalty and were ushered to a table. We ate supper at the Supper Club and were given many smiles and nods from the Oneida veterans. What a warm welcome, I thought.

I noticed how well the veterans got along with each other; the feeling of camaraderie was as tall as a parachute flare and was as wide as a 155 mm artillery shell. Some veterans told me they had seen and heard me when I was at LZ Lambeau. One even told me I was the star of that show at Lambeau Field.

Our table was selected to go first through the chow line, and, of course, I had to buy some 50/50 raffle tickets on the way by.

I stood up and told some stories about my time in the military and recited poetry about my time in the Vietnam War and afterward. I could tell my words were resonating with the Oneida veterans. I felt like I was related to the veterans there, even the not-so-pretty ones. There were young veterans, old veterans, female veterans, and family members.

I would gladly go back to Green Bay and visit with the veterans there anytime.

After the doings, we went back to the casino, where we had some modest wins on the slot machines. I noticed the difference between their casino and our casino. There, a lot of people dress up for a night at the casino: slinky dresses and high heels on the women, suits and sport coats for the men. At our casino, there were not as many dressed like that.

We motored home with a full tank of gas and full smiles on our faces. The warm welcome will be long remembered.

NOTICE to the Tuscon Unified School District:

I have checked your list of banned books and cannot find any of my titles there. I am hoping someone can take care of this oversight.

My titles are: 1) *Walking the Rez Road*, 1993, Voyageur Press; 2) *The Rez Road Follies: Canoes, Casinos, Computers, and Birch Bark Baskets*, 1997, Kodansha Press, reprinted by the University of Minnesota Press; 3) *Anishinaabe Syndicated*, 2011, Minnesota Historical Society Press; and 4) *Rez Salute: The Real Healer Dealer*, due out fall 2012, Fulcrum Publishing. Just for background information, I have been writing the Fond du Lac Follies for newspapers for more than twenty-two years. I have written opinion pieces for other newspapers and have also written two plays.

I am Anishinaabe, a member of the Fond du Lac Band of Lake Superior Chippewa, enrollment #3166. I live on the Fond du Lac Reservation, established by the Treaty of 1854 in what is now called Minnesota.

My grandfather Joseph A. Northrup was also an author, and I can't find his name on your list of banned books. Among other materials, he wrote a book called *Wawina* back in the 1930s. He was also a member of the Fond du Lac Band of Lake Superior Chippewa. Would you please consider banning his book also?

Your assistance in this matter would be greatly appreciated.

About the Author

© Ivy Vainio

Jim Northrup is an award-winning journalist, poet, and playwright. His syndicated column, Fond du Lac Follies, was named Best Column at the 1999 Native American Journalists Association convention, and he holds an honorary doctorate of letters from Fond du Lac Tribal and Community College.